People of Destiny

A Humanities Series

There comes a time,
we know not when,
that marks
the destiny of men.

Joseph Addison Alexander

People of Destiny

SIR WINSTON CHURCHILL

By Kenneth G. Richards

Robert Ratcliffe, Ph.D., historical adviser

CHILDRENS PRESS, CHICAGO

The editors wish to express their appreciation to Mr. Meyer Goldberg, who created the series and inspired the publication of People of Destiny

Cover and body design: John Hollis

Project editor: Joan Downing

Editorial assistant: Gerri Stoller

Illustrations: Bob Brunton, Nita Engle—Hollis Associates

Research editor: Robert Hendrickson

Photographs: From the files of Wide World Photos, Inc., the Radio Times Hulton Picture Library, the Imperial War Museum, the Bettman Archive, Aerofilms Ltd., Culver Pictures, Paris Match, Reuters, Central Press, London News Agency Photos Ltd., Camera Press, Mirrorpic, and Mr. Cecil Beaton.

Typesetting: American Typesetting Co.

Printing: The Regensteiner Corporation

Quotations on pages 12; 13; 55, col. 1, ll. 43-47; 55, col. 2; 56; 58; 59; 60; 62; 64; 66; 68; 69; 71; 72; 75; 76; and 79 from The Second World War, *by Winston Churchill, published in Boston by Houghton Mifflin Company and in London by Cassell and Company Ltd., 1948-1953.*
Quotations on pages 19; 20; 22; 24, col. 2, ll. 2-4, 9-10, 12-16, and 24-26; 31; and 39, col. 2 from My Early Life, A Roving Commission, *by Winston Churchill, published in New York by Charles Scribner's Sons and in London by Odhams Books Ltd., 1930.*
Quotations on pages 38, col. 2, ll. 26-32 and 39, col. 1 from Winston Churchill: An Informal Study of Greatness, *by Robert Lewis Taylor, Doubleday & Company, Inc., New York, 1952.*
Quotations on pages 81 and 84 from Man of the Century, *by the editors of Readers Digest, copyright © 1965 by the Readers Digest Association, Inc., by permission of Little, Brown and Co.*
Quotation on page 24, col. 2, ll. 29-32 from Winston Churchill, the Era and the Man, *by Virginia Cowles, Harper & Row, Publishers, Incorporated, New York, 1953.*
Quotation on page 55, col. 1, ll. 11-14 from Portraits in Power, *by S. E. Ayling, Barnes & Noble, Inc., New York, 1963.*

Library of Congress Catalog Card No. 67-26874

Contents

The Call of Destiny

An expectant wave of murmuring ran through the House of Commons on this thirteenth day of May, 1940. Called to a special session at the request of the new Prime Minister, the Members of Parliament anxiously awaited his appearance. For the first time in his new post, Winston Churchill was about to speak to the assembled House. He would request a vote of confidence in the new administration he was forming. He would need their unanimous support to carry on in the trying months ahead.

In the more than eight months since war had been declared following Hitler's attack on Poland, the British Parliament had expressed an increasing dissatisfaction with Prime Minister Neville Chamberlain. In the years of the gathering storm, Chamberlain carried on a policy of appeasement to German demands. The final humility in the name of peace came at Munich on September 29, 1938, as Chamberlain and the French Premier, Daladier, signed away to Hitler some 5,000,000 inhabitants and 16,000 square miles of Czechoslovakia. There were no Czechoslovakian representatives at the meeting.

On May 10, 1940, Prime Minister Neville Chamberlain (below center) stepped down from office and Winston Churchill became chief head of state. In the more than eight months since war had been declared following Adolf Hitler's attack on Poland, the British Parliament had expressed an increasing dissatisfaction with Chamberlain. In the years of the gathering storm, when German troops marched across Europe invading and occupying much of the country (below), Chamberlain carried on a policy of appeasement to German demands. With the outbreak of war, he worked as hard for victory as he had for peace, but he lacked the confidence of many Members of Parliament and his effectiveness diminished as the headlines grew more ominous.

Chamberlain arrived back in London waving a "peace pact" stating that the paper, signed by Hitler, meant "peace in our time." Subsequent events proved otherwise and on March 31, 1939, the British and French belatedly pledged support to Poland in the event of further German expansion attempts. With the outbreak of war on September 1, 1939, Chamberlain worked as ardently for victory as he had for peace. He lacked the confidence of many Members of Parliament, however, and his effectiveness diminished as the headlines grew more ominous.

In April of 1940 Hitler occupied Denmark and invaded Norway. Though British and French expeditionary forces went immediately to the aid of the stricken country, after initial victories they soon found themselves being pushed into the sea. This proved more than the House members could accept and in a stormy debate on the seventh of May they made it abundantly clear that Chamberlain lacked their confidence.

Churchill, who was then First Lord of the Admiralty and a member of Chamberlain's war cabinet, wound up

the debate with an impassioned and loyal defense of his chief. In the ensuing voting, however, over fifty of Chamberlain's own party voted with the opposition. It was now obvious that, for the sake of the nation, a new leader had to be found.

On May 10, Neville Chamberlain stepped down as Prime Minister. At six o'clock that evening, Churchill was summoned to Buckingham Palace to see King George VI, who appointed him Prime Minister. After forty years in Parliament, Winston Churchill, sixty-five years old, now became the chief head of state.

If the skies had been dark on the days of the debate, they suddenly turned darker still. On the very morning of Churchill's appointment as Prime Minister, the German forces had launched an unprovoked, surprise attack against neutral Holland, Belgium, and Luxembourg. By daybreak more than seventy Nazi divisions were pouring across the frontiers of the Low Countries. The terror of the *Blitzkrieg* was felt in these countries as it had been felt the previous fall in Poland. Great new burdens were already heaped upon the new Prime Minister.

That evening, Churchill met with the leaders of the Labour and Liberal parties and asked them to join in a National Government. That is, all three political parties would lay aside bipartisan views and all would share the responsibilities of government under Churchill's leadership. They readily agreed, and before midnight Churchill had sent the King a list of the first five members he had selected for his war cabinet.

The self-confidence of Churchill is best expressed in his own words. As he later wrote in his history of the Second World War, "I was conscious of a profound sense of relief. At last I had the authority to give directions over the whole scene. I felt as if I were walking with Destiny, and that all my past life had been but a preparation for this hour and for this trial. . . . I thought I knew a good deal about it all, and I was sure I should not fail. Therefore, although impatient for the morning, I slept soundly and had no need for cheering dreams. Facts are better than dreams."

Throughout the weekend of May 11 and 12, Churchill labored to form a government in the wake of new disasters on the continent. The German onslaught was rolling unchecked along the roads of the Low Countries and by Monday morning German soldiers were within twenty-five miles of Brussels. French and British armies rushing to the aid of the Dutch and Belgians often did not have a chance to form a defense line before the *Panzers* were upon them. It was under this grave situation that Churchill went to make his speech before the House of Commons.

At last the familiar, robust, slightly stooped figure appeared walking briskly to the podium. As he stood before them, the assembly may well have taken a second look at the man who not so long ago had been considered a sort of rabble-rouser and prophet of doom. The dark eyes that darted quickly about the chamber reflected the fire of vitality and the pent-up energy that burned within him. The eyebrows, always seeming to scowl when his mood was serious, bespoke the intensity and seriousness with which he grasped the supreme power of the state. The pouting lower lip and firm set of the jaw announced a confidence, tenacity, and determination that left no room for doubt or weakness. He exuded all the majesty and pride of the British lion, the unflagging courage of the English bulldog, and an all abid-

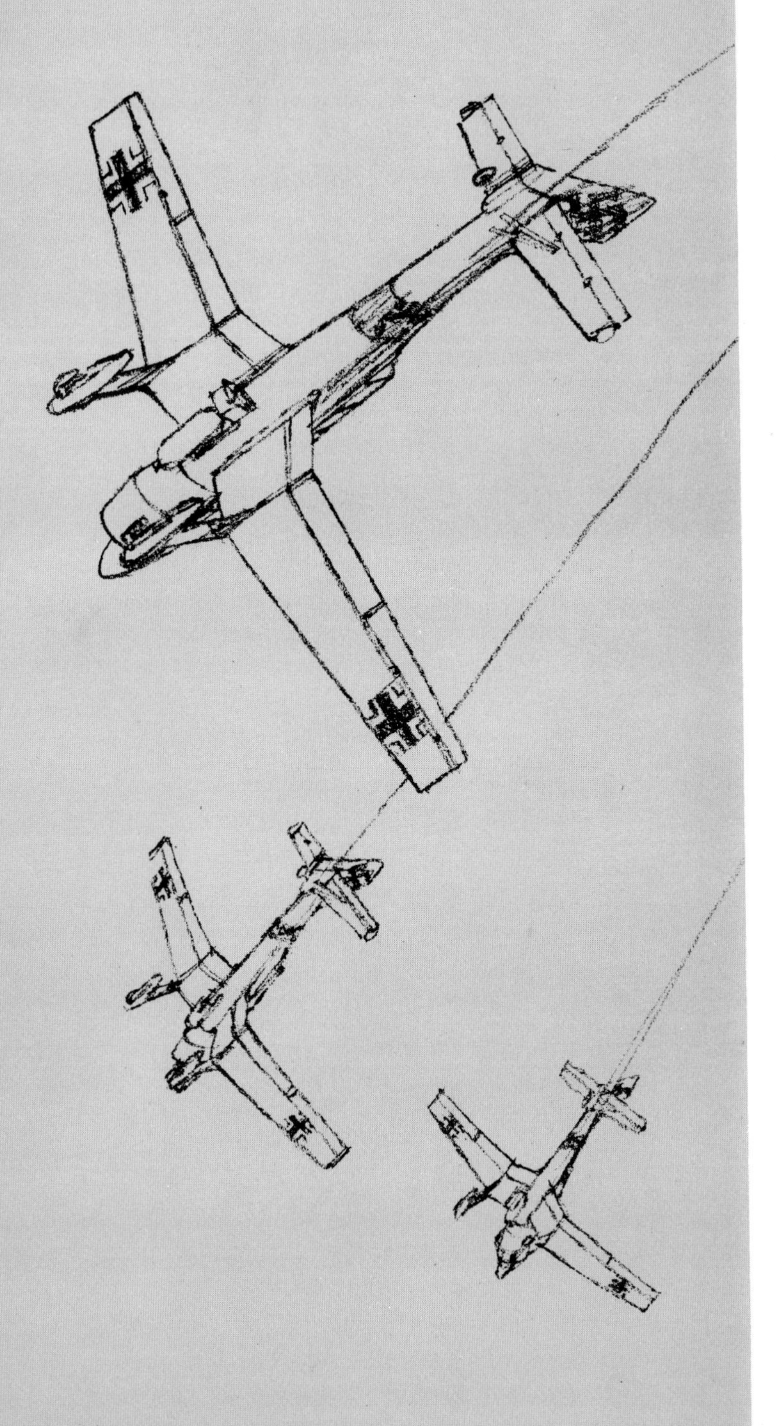

On the very morning of Churchill's appointment as Prime Minister, the German forces had launched an attack against neutral Holland, Belgium, and Luxembourg. The terror of the Blitzkrieg *was felt in these countries as it had been felt the previous fall in Poland. First came waves of dive bombers, or* Stukas *(above),* followed by *armored tank divisions, or* Panzers, *smashing holes in the enemy lines.*

ing faith in the ideals and purpose of the British Empire.

A hush fell over the chamber as he began with an explanation of why he had called this special meeting and continued with a report of the progress he had made in filling the various cabinet offices. As for himself he said, "I have nothing to offer but blood, toil, tears, and sweat." Then he stated the policy and aims he was setting for his country.

"You ask, what is our policy? I will say: It is to wage war, by sea, land, and air, with all our might and with all the strength that God can give us: to wage war against a monstrous tyranny, never surpassed in the dark, lamentable catalogue of human crime. That is our policy.

"You ask, what is our aim? I can answer in one word: Victory—victory at all costs, victory in spite of all terror; victory however long and hard the road may be; for without victory, there is no survival. . . . But I take up my task with buoyancy and hope. I feel sure that our cause will not be suffered to fail among men. At this time I feel entitled to claim the aid of all, and I say, 'Come, then, let us go forward together with our united strength.' " The House roared its unanimous approval.

Thus ended the first of Winston Churchill's speeches as Prime Minister. In the dark years ahead before the tide could be turned, when England's cities lay in smoldering ruins, and in the face of defeats in many far-flung corners of the globe, the beautiful, fierce, and defiant words of their leader were often the only hope and inspiration to which the British people could turn. But here, in May, 1940, Winston Churchill began his walk with destiny with a united Parliament, a determined people, and a complete faith in the justice of their cause. The call of destiny was answered.

Fourth Form Boy

"On the 30th of November at Blenheim Palace, the Lady Randolph Churchill, prematurely, of a son."

This one line in the London *Times* announced the birth of Winston Leonard Spencer Churchill at Blenheim Palace, his family home, in 1874. No mention was made that the event occurred in a small cloakroom filled with silk hats and velvet capes. In the ballroom nearby, a gala St. Andrew's Day Ball had been in progress when the baby's mother was suddenly rushed from the festivities to the nearest available room of comfort and privacy. Thus, young Winston's very arrival in the world was fraught with crisis and expediency.

The first Churchill about whom anything much is known was the son of a lawyer and the grandson of a blacksmith. Like his famous descendent, he was a soldier, a writer, and a Member of Parliament. He married a relative of Sir Frances Drake and produced three remarkable children. One was John Churchill, the first Duke of Marlborough (1650–1722), who proved himself one of the greatest soldiers of all time.

After Marlborough's great victory at Blenheim in 1704, Queen Anne made him a gift of 1500 acres at Woodstock, a few miles from the city of Oxford, and Parliament approved the sum of 24,000 pounds for the building of Blenheim Palace, designed by the architect Sir John Vanbrugh.

Blenheim, one of the great houses of England, has for nearly three centuries served as the official residence of the Dukes of Marlborough. In 1950, the Great Hall and the West Wing of the palace were opened to the public. Blenheim's greatest tourist attraction, however, is neither its architecture nor its splendid interior trappings. Rather, it is the fact that the palace served as the birthplace of Sir Winston Churchill.

The first Duke of Marlborough had no sons, and Winston is descended through the Duke's daughter Anne, wife of Charles, Lord Spencer. Thus his

---

One of Winston Churchill's ancestors was John Churchill, the first Duke of Marlborough (opposite top), who proved himself one of the greatest soldiers of all time. After his great victory at Blenheim in 1704, Queen Anne made him a gift of land on which was built Blenheim Palace, one of the great houses of England (opposite bottom). This magnificent palace served as the birthplace of Winston Churchill on November 30, 1874.

true family name is Spencer. In 1817, however, the fourth Duke of Marlborough received royal permission to add the name Churchill to perpetuate the surname of the first Duke. Many members of the family still prefer the hyphenated version of Spencer-Churchill.

Winston's father, Lord Randolph Churchill, was considered by many to be the most brilliant politician of his age. A Member of Parliament at the time of Winston's birth, he was later to serve as Chancellor of the Exchequer and Leader of the House of Commons.

On his mother's side, Winston was American. As a matter of fact, he was part Iroquois Indian.

Winston's mother, who was named for the famous singer Jenny Lind, was the great-granddaughter of Reuben Murray, a lieutenant in George Washington's Continental Army. In later years, Sir Winston received with great pride the honor of membership in the Society of Cincinnati, an organization of men descended from officers who served in the Revolution.

Lord Randolph Churchill, Winston's father, was twenty-four when he met his bride, nineteen-year-old Jennie Jerome, in Europe in the summer of 1873. They were introduced at a ball; the next night he went to dinner with her; and the third evening he proposed and she accepted.

A talented young woman of striking beauty, with dark flashing eyes, a charming personality, and exceptional poise, Jennie was invariably admired in fashionable society. She loved festive events, and it was against the advice of her doctors that she attended the St. Andrew's Day Ball at Blenheim Palace on that memorable night of November 30, 1874.

The year Winston was born was a quiet one. The Franco–Prussian War was now ended, and Europe was once again engaged in peaceful pursuits. A Frenchman by the name of Auguste Bartholdi was busy working on plans for a great monument to Franco–American friendship to be called the Statue of Liberty. Thus the bonds between the Old World and the New were being strengthened.

Little would anyone guess that the robust infant, Winston Spencer Churchill, would someday be called upon to forge new and stronger bonds between the two worlds. The baby, born in a cloakroom, would someday stride the halls of most of the great governmental institutions of the world. The Old World and the New were mingled in his blood and both played a part in his making.

Before Winston was two years old, his family moved to Ireland where his father was secretary to Winston's grandfather.

Lord Randolph Churchill, Winston's father, was twenty-four when he met his bride, nineteen-year-old Jennie Jerome (opposite), in Europe in the summer of 1873. They were introduced at a ball; the next night he went to dinner with her; and the third evening he proposed.

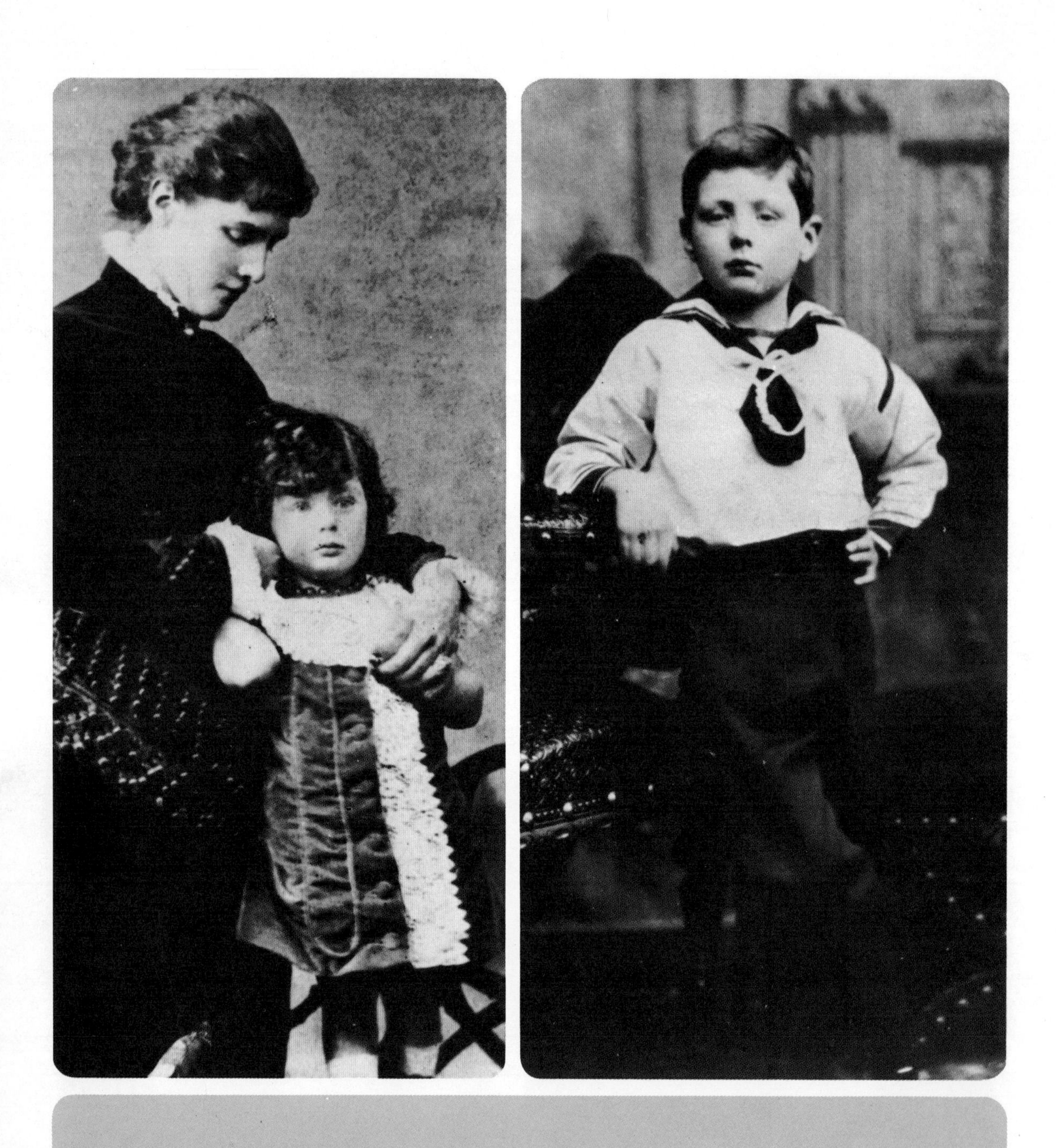

Winston Churchill is shown at the age of two with his mother (above left). Above right, he is seven years old, at which age he was sent off to St. James' School. This was an unhappy chapter in his life. He hated the school, and after two years, his parents took him away.

"I did what so many oppressed peoples have done in similar circumstances: I took to the woods . . ."

It was here that, as Winston put it, he was "first menaced with Education. The approach of a sinister figure described as 'the Governess' was announced. . . . When the fateful hour struck and the Governess was due to arrive . . . I did what so many oppressed peoples have done in similar circumstances: I took to the woods. . . . Hours passed before I was retrieved . . ." Winston would never be a great scholar.

Winston was dismayed that his mother "almost always" sided with the Governess. His mother "shone for me like the Evening Star. I loved her dearly—but at a distance." As was the custom among wealthy families of Victorian England, the children were left to the care of a "nanny," or nurse. The parents—and Winston's were no exception—remained rather remote and aloof from their children and moved about in their own world of society.

Winston was fortunate in having for a nanny a Mrs. Everest, who loved the red-headed, freckled youngster almost as her own. "My nurse was my confidante," Winston would write in later years. "Mrs. Everest it was who looked after me and tended all my wants. It was to her I poured out my many troubles . . ."

In 1880 Winston's brother John was born, and the family returned to England. Winston was sent off to St. James' School, "one of the most fashionable and expensive in the country. I was no more consulted about leaving home than I had been about coming into the world," he wrote later. Still, "I thought in spite of the lessons, it would be fun living with so many other boys, and that we should make friends together and have great adventures." He described himself at this stage of his life as "what grown-up people in their offhand way called 'a troublesome boy.' "

It was a dark November day when Winston's mother deposited him at the school. By now the seven-year-old was beginning to feel "miserable at the idea of being left alone among all these strangers in this great, fierce, formidable place." It was to prove an unhappy chapter in the life of Winston Churchill.

"How I hated this school, and what a life of anxiety I lived there for more than two years," Winston remembered later. "I made very little progress at my lessons, and none at all at games. I counted the days and the hours to the end of every term, when I should return home from this hateful servitude."

The headmaster of the school was a cruel person and Winston got his share and more of the floggings he administered. It was in this school that his basic qualities of independence and stubborn defiance in the face of adversity which were to mark his life in later years first came to the fore. Despite the threat of the birch rod, Winston refused to be cowed by the headmaster. He refused to surrender; he refused to curry favor; he refused to repent. Once, to the delight of the other students, he even kicked the headmaster's straw hat to pieces. But in time, "I fell into a low state of health at St. James' School, and finally my parents took me away."

For the next three years Winston attended a school at Brighton where, he said, "I was allowed to learn things which interested me: French, History, lots of Poetry by heart, and above all, Riding and Swimming." This was a happy period for Winston despite a bout with double pneumonia.

By now Lord Randolph was at the zenith of his meteoric political career, and Winston began a scrapbook of his father's activities as Chancellor of the Exchequer and Leader of the House of Commons. Winston was intensely proud of his father and yet his father remained, for the most part, unapproachable. It was during this period that Winston became interested in politics and on his days at home from school had many occasions to meet some of his father's statesman friends, including Prime Minister Disraeli.

When he was twelve, Winston entered Harrow, a well-known English boys' school. It was here, he would write later, that "I got into my bones the essential structure of the ordinary British sentence—which is a noble thing." He refused to learn Latin or Greek, and as a consequence remained in the lower segment of his class. But another consequence was that he had three times more English than the others, and, as history now testifies, he learned it completely and thoroughly.

As in his previous schools, Winston continued to be a rather poor student at Harrow as well. "I was in due course placed in the third, or lowest, division of the Fourth, or bottom, Form." As he wrote later, "I was on the whole considerably discouraged by my school days. It is not pleasant to feel oneself so completely outclassed and left behind at the very beginning of the race." Despite being "stagnated in the lowest form," however, Winston developed a prodigious memory and once won a prize for reciting 1200 lines of Macaulay's *Lays* without a single mistake.

One day, when Winston was at home on holiday from Harrow, his father

---

When he was twelve, Winston entered Harrow, a well-known English boys' school. As in his previous schools, Winston continued to be a rather poor student, but he did develop a remarkable memory. Opposite, he is shown in 1889, after he had been at Harrow for three years.

*"I got into my bones
the essential structure
of the ordinary
English sentence—
which is a noble thing."*

happened to walk in and find the boy's army of 1500 toy soldiers arrayed in an attack position on the battlefield. "He spent twenty minutes studying the scene—which was really impressive—with a keen eye and captivating smile. At the end he asked me if I would like to go into the army . . . . I said 'Yes' at once; and immediately I was taken at my word. . . . Henceforward all my education was directed to passing into Sandhurst . . ."

It took Winston three tries to pass the examinations before he was finally accepted into the Royal Military College at Sandhurst. Following his second failure, Winston left Harrow and began a special "crammers course" to prepare himself for a final try. He very nearly never got the chance to try again. While on a Christmas holiday he met with a serious accident which nearly ended his life.

While playing a game, he tried to avoid being captured by his brother and a cousin, and leaped from a bridge hoping to catch the branches of a tree. He missed, however, and fell twenty-nine feet to the ground. Unconscious for several days, and with a ruptured kidney, among other injuries, he was fortunate to have survived at all.

But survive he did, and while convalescing in London, he made frequent visits to the House of Commons to listen to the parliamentary debates. Mr. William E. Gladstone was once again Prime Minister of Great Britain—the Liberals having come to power in the summer of 1892. This was also the year that Grover Cleveland was elected, for the second time, President of the United States. He was to appoint Mr. Thomas Bayard as the first United States Ambassador to Great Britain in 1893. Another event of lesser note in that year of 1893 occurred when Winston Churchill at last passed his entrance examination and was admitted to Sandhurst.

In 1893, Winston Churchill passed his entrance examination and was admitted to the Royal Military College at Sandhurst. Opposite, Winston in his Sandhurst uniform.

A Soldier of the Queen

Winston loved Sandhurst. "I had a new start," he wrote in later years. "I was no longer handicapped by past neglect of Latin, French, or Mathematics. We had now to learn fresh things and we all started equal. Tactics, Fortification, Topography (mapmaking), Military Law, and Military Administration formed the whole curriculum. In addition were Drill, Gymnastics, and Riding. Discipline was strict and the hours of study and parade were long. One was very tired at the end of the day."

It was during his stay at Sandhurst that he developed his closest relationship, however tenuous, with his remote and distant father. He was allowed to accompany Lord Randolph to the theater and the races on occasion, "But if ever I began to show the slightest idea of comradeship, he was immediately offended; and when once I suggested that I might help his private secretary write some of his letters, he froze me into stone."

Nonetheless, Winston always continued hoping to break the barrier between himself and his father. About the rebukes he received from Lord Randolph while at Sandhurst he would say, "I know now that this would have been only a passing phase." With almost childlike naïveté Winston would convince himself in later years that, "Had he lived another four or five years, he could not have done without me."

The time passed swiftly and in December of 1894, Winston graduated from Sandhurst standing eighth in his class of 150. "It showed," he would write later, "that I could learn quickly enough the things that mattered."

On the following January 24, Winston's father died. He had been a sick man for some time. Though he took little interest in his son's affairs he did seem "quite willing, and even pleased, that I should become a Cavalry Officer." With his father's death, Winston said, "All my dreams of comradeship with him, of entering Parliament at his side and in his support were ended. There remained for me only to pursue his aims and vindicate his memory."

Six months later, Winston received another blow. His beloved nurse, Mrs. Everest, passed away. When Winston heard that she was seriously ill he traveled to London to see her and to arrange for two specialist doctors to attend her. But it was to no avail. She died quietly and easily. "She had been my dearest and most intimate friend during the whole of the twenty years I had lived," Winston remembered. After her death, Winston quoted a passage from Gibbon as her epitaph: "If there be any, as I trust there are some, who rejoice that I live, to that dear and excellent woman their gratitude is due." In later years, when he had become one of the world's great figures, Mrs. Everest's picture still hung over his desk.

In March of 1895, Winston was commissioned a lieutenant in the Queen's Fourth Hussars, then stationed at Aldershot. For the first six months he was

Winston loved Sandhurst, where he learned tactics, fortification, topography, military law, and military administration. The time passed swiftly and he was graduated in December, 1894. In March, 1895, he was commissioned a lieutenant in the Queen's Fourth Hussars (left.)

given recruit's training along with the troopers. The training was tough, hard, and bruising. But Winston was a tough and hardened young man and with his deep-seated pluck and tenacity, managed to survive the rigors of the cavalry.

He longed, however, for real adventure and a taste of danger. The whole world seemed to be at peace but Winston discovered that there was some guerrilla fighting going on in Cuba. Accordingly, he took leave of his regiment and sailed to Havana in early November of 1895. Before leaving, he made arrangements to write articles for the *Daily Graphic* about his adventures.

In Cuba, Churchill got his first taste of battle as the rebels attacked the Spanish army unit to which he was attached. The action was limited to small skirmishes but Churchill was satisfied.

He sailed home from Cuba to find his regiment preparing to go to India. There was trouble brewing among the tribesmen on India's northwest frontier. When Winston's regiment arrived in India in 1896, instead of getting into battle they spent their time at Bangalore playing polo or cards and leading a very quiet life. It was here in Bangalore at the age of twenty-two that the desire for learning came upon Winston Churchill, and with it his first real impulse to educate himself.

He ordered books from England and, during the long, hot afternoons while others slept, he read Macaulay, Gibbon, Darwin, Mathus, Plato's *Republic*, the *Politics* of Aristotle, and Bartlett's *Familiar Quotations*. He read with a hunger, not from habit or from duty but from need, and he absorbed these books in both style and content.

In 1897 he returned to England on leave. He had not been home very long when news came of a new revolt among the Pathan tribesmen on the Indian frontier. He immediately telegraphed Sir Bindon Blood, the commander being sent to subdue the uprising, for permission to join the expedition. Then, without waiting for a reply, he caught the next ship for India. The General's reply caught Winston at Bombay. It read: "Very difficult; no vacancies; come up as a correspondent; will try to fit you in. B.B."

Winston had already taken the trouble to get commissions from the Allahabad *Pioneer* and the London *Daily Telegraph;* leave was quickly granted from his own regiment. He immediately reported to the Malakand Field Force, which was already engaged in fighting in the Himalayan passes.

After several battles and skirmishes, the expedition up the Mamund Valley was successfully completed. Sir Bindon Blood praised Winston in dispatches. Having tasted his first real battle, Winston was eager for more but he was only unofficially attached to the expedition and soon had to return to his own regiment at Bangalore.

Now in his spare time he wrote his first book, an account of the frontier war entitled, *The Malakand Field Force,* which was an immediate success. When the first published volume reached him, together with a shower of critical acclaim, he was filled with pride and pleasure. One letter that gave him "extreme pleasure" came from the Prince of Wales, later King Edward VII, who offered his congratulations on the success of the book.

The fighting on the Indian frontier gradually dwindled and soon sputtered out as prolonged peace negotiations took place. Peace descended upon India and boredom upon the eager Churchill. Then new fighting broke out in the Sudan where Sir Herbert Kitchener was opening a campaign to drive some 200

In 1896, Churchill's regiment arrived in India, where the picture opposite was taken. Instead of getting into battle they spent their time at Bangalore playing polo or cards and leading a very quiet life. Here, at the age of twenty-two, the desire for learning came upon Winston. He ordered books from England and read and absorbed them in both style and content.

miles southward to Omdurman, the Dervish capital, where a decisive battle was expected to be fought. Winston immediately applied to join Kitchener's army but was quickly refused. Undaunted by this rebuke, Churchill took leave of his regiment in India and sailed for London. There he solicited and received the support of Prime Minister Lord Salisbury. His mother, Lady Randolph, used her persuasive charms to win the Adjutant General, Sir Evelyn Wood, to her son's cause. Two days later he received orders to report as a supernumerary lieutenant to the Twenty-first Lancers in Cairo. The next morning he caught a train for Marseilles. Before leaving he made arrangements to write a series of letters to the *Morning Post.*

And so, in August of 1898, Lieutenant Churchill arrived in Cairo just as the regiment was starting up the Nile. A month later he reached the battlefront in time to participate in what was to be the last of the classic cavalry charges of history. The charge resembled in some ways the famous Charge of the Light Brigade at Balaclava, Russia. Three hundred Lancers rode at the gallop to crash headlong into a waiting line of some 3000 Dervishes. Losses were heavy but the Churchill luck held and Winston came out unscathed. Three days after the battle, Winston sailed down the Nile, homeward bound for London.

In 1898, Churchill joined Sir Herbert Kitchener's Twenty-first Lancers in Cairo just as the regiment was starting up the Nile on the way to Omdurman, the Dervish capital of the Sudan, where a decisive battle was expected to be fought. He reached the battlefront in time to participate in what was to be the last of the classic cavalry charges of history. Three hundred Lancers rode at the gallop to crash headlong into a waiting line of some 3 000 Dervishes (left).

Winston Churchill was to participate in one more war before launching a career in politics. In October of 1899, the Boer War began in South Africa. Churchill sailed for South Africa with a commission as special correspondent for the Morning Post. *The photograph below was taken during the Boer War.*

During the voyage, Winston began work on a new book called *The River War,* in which he described the campaign just completed. It was to receive even greater critical acclaim than his previous work.

As the final year of the nineteenth century rolled around, Winston resigned from the army that no longer seemed to hold out the challenge a career in journalism offered. At about the same time he took his first fling in politics.

In England one is not required to be a resident of the constituency in which one stands for election. Accordingly, Winston entered the Conservative ranks and, in October, 1899, ran for a seat in the House of Commons as the representative from Oldham, an industrial town in Lancashire. When all the votes were tallied, Winston had been roundly defeated by more than a thousand votes. "I returned to London," he would remember, "with those feelings of deflation which a bottle of champagne or even soda water represent when it has been half emptied and left uncorked overnight." But he received encouragement from no less than Mr. Balfour, then Leader of the House of Commons, who wrote: "Never mind, it will all come right; and this small reverse will have no permanent ill effect upon your political fortunes." This proved to be a most prophetic statement.

There was one more war to participate in before launching a career in politics, however. In that October of 1899, the Boer War began in South Africa. Winston was offered a commission as special correspondent for the *Morning Post,* which he quickly accepted at the princely salary of 250 pounds per month (about $1200) plus all expenses. He sailed on the eleventh of October on the steamer *Dunottar Castle,* and within two weeks after his arrival found himself a prisoner of war.

Winston's troubles began on the morning of November 15, when he rode out on a reconnoitering sortie in an armored train. They had gone about fourteen miles when they were surprised by a band of Boers armed with a cannon. The train, which also carried a company of Dublin Fusiliers and another of Durban Light Infantry, was quickly taken under fire and three of the cars were derailed.

Winston jumped from the train as bullets whistled and ricocheted off the armor plate. Calling for volunteers to help clear the track, Winston soon had the engine freed. It took more than an hour to complete the job, and all the while the Boers poured an unrelenting fire of bullets and shells upon the harassed British. It was decided to load the wounded into the engine and let the others walk beside the train on the side protected from the Boer guns.

The train moved too fast, however, for the walking men to keep up and was soon some 300 yards ahead of the men. Churchill, who was in the cab, ordered the train stopped, climbed down, and went back to find the soldiers. Instead he was met by Boer riflemen who aimed and fired. The bullets whistled past Winston and kicked up little tufts of dust. Leaping over the six-foot bank of the railroad bed, it seemed for a brief moment that he was free—the Blue Krantz River and pos-

On November 15, 1899, Churchill rode out on a reconnoitering sortie in an armored train. After traveling about fourteen miles, they were surprised by a band of Boers armed with a cannon (illustration). The train was quickly taken under fire and three of the cars were derailed.

sible escape lay only yards away. As Winston broke for the river, a Boer rifleman on horseback overtook him. Unarmed as he was, Winston had no alternative but to surrender.

Taken to Pretoria, Churchill was imprisoned along with some sixty British officers. But prison life was not for him. On the night of December 12, he scaled a wall of the prison and then walked boldly across a lawn, past an armed sentry, and through the outer gate to freedom. Once again the Churchill audacity served him well.

By dawn his escape was known and soon a printed notice offering a reward of twenty-five pounds for his return—dead or alive—was being circulated. But Winston had hopped aboard a freight train and, though still in the heart of enemy country, was putting miles between himself and Pretoria. Before daylight, he jumped from the train and continued on foot. As the Churchill luck would have it, he stumbled into the hands of an Englishman—the only friend in miles—who hid the escaped prisoner in the bottom of a mine. After hiding in this uncomfortable place for five nights, Winston was smuggled aboard a train and hidden amid huge bales of wool. A three-day journey in these dismal accommodations brought Winston to Lourenço Marques, in Portuguese territory. From there he caught a steamship to Durban where he learned that his exploits had made him famous. He was quickly back on his job as war correspondent and spent Christmas Eve in a hut within 100 yards of where he had been captured little more than a month before.

Winston also rejoined the army for a brief period and took part in the relief expedition of Ladysmith, battles in the Orange Free State, and the fighting in the Transvaal. From his experiences in these actions came the material for two books, *London to Ladysmith* and *Ian Hamilton's March*. In June of 1900, Winston sailed home to England.

And so ended, for the moment, the military life of Winston Churchill. He returned home to find himself a popular hero who was known throughout the country. Elections were once again being held in England and the twenty-five-year-old hero found nearly a dozen constituencies soliciting his candidacy. He could have chosen one that offered the best prospects of victory. Instead, he chose to run once again in Oldham, the scene of his defeat the year before. This time the results would be different and Winston Churchill would begin a political career unparalleled in history.

Shortly after the attack on the train, Churchill was overtaken by a Boer rifleman on horseback and was forced to surrender. He was taken to Pretoria and imprisoned along with some sixty British officers (opposite, top). Prison life was not for Winston, however, and on the night of December 12, he scaled a wall of the prison (opposite bottom), walked boldly across a lawn past an armed sentry, and through the outer gate to freedom.

The Rise and Fall of a Politician

In those days, at the turn of the century, elections in England were held over a period of nearly six weeks. The first results to be announced were likely to have a decided influence upon subsequent polls. For that reason, the results at Oldham, one of the first constituencies to conduct its election, were watched with interest throughout the nation.

Foreign affairs—the Boer War in particular—was the principal issue in the elections that year. Winston's widely acclaimed activities in South Africa served him well, for he could speak of the action from personal experience. When the results were finally tallied, Winston had won and the success of the eloquent young man did much to assure his party's return to power. Winston was now a rising star in British politics.

Four days after the opening of Parliament, Winston rose to make his maiden speech before the House of

Churchill participated in several battles of the Boer War, and from his experiences in these actions drew material for two books. In June of 1900, he sailed home for England. He returned home to find himself a popular hero who was known throughout the country. Elections were once again being held, and Churchill ran in Oldham (below), the scene of his defeat the year before. When the results were tallied, he had won. This was to be the beginning of a political career unparalleled in history.

On September 12, 1908, Winston took one of the most important steps of his life. He took as his bride the lovely Miss Clementine Hozier, daughter of Colonel and Lady Blanche Hozier of Dundee. The wedding was one of the social events of the year. Despite the opinions of some that the marriage would not last, it was to become one of the happiest and most-enduring romances of the century. As Winston put it: "I married and lived happily ever afterwards." In the photographs at right, the couple are shown on their wedding day.

Commons. As a rule, new members of the House, and especially young ones, were expected to sit quietly for several weeks, or even months, and watch and listen to the older members. Even his father, Lord Randolph, had waited two months before making his maiden speech. But the brash, twenty-six-year-old Winston had things that needed saying. The subject of the current debate was the war in South Africa and Winston had more firsthand experience with that conflict than any other member of the House.

Winston had worked long and hard in preparing his speech, which he committed to memory. It was an eloquent oration and was well received by the members, who traditionally attach considerable weight to graceful rhetoric. Winston ended the speech with a reference to his father. "I cannot sit down," he said, "without saying how grateful I am for the kindness and patience with which the House has heard me. It has been extended to me, I well know, not on my own account, but because of a splendid memory which many old members still preserve."

Joseph Chamberlain, whose own son Neville would someday become Prime Minister of England, found in the speech an indication "that we may see the father repeated in the son."

And so began a parliamentary career that would span more than sixty years. Almost from the very beginning, Winston demonstrated a willingness to attack any bill, any proposal, any concept, or any person who differed with his own views. He would never be classified as a party hack. The fierce independence and self-confidence of his early youth was undeterred by the formidable and august surroundings of the House of Commons. His great combative spirit was made-to-order for the cut and thrust of parliamentary debate.

He soon became the *enfant terrible* of the House of Commons. He developed a wit that was alternately biting and humorous, feared and admired. Few men or institutions were immune to the Churchillian barbs or jests. Once he sat vigorously shaking his head in disagreement with a member who was making an address before the House.

"I see," cried the speaker, "my right honorable friend shaking his head. I wish to remind him that I am only expressing my own opinion."

"And I wish to remind the speaker," Churchill rejoined, "that I am only shaking my own head!"

On another occasion he said of a fellow member, "he can be described as one of those orators who, before they get up, do not know what they are going to say; when they are speaking, do not know what they are saying; and, when they have sat down, do not know what they have said."

Winston reveled in banter and repartee. He could appreciate a point well delivered even if he were the target. In the course of his long political career his sense of humor would serve him well, for he was often to become the target of both good-natured jests and vitriolic diatribes.

Winston soon fell out of sorts with his own Conservative party. His belief in free trade and social reform led to a growing rift between himself and Joseph Chamberlain and Prime Minister Balfour. Finally, on May 31, 1903, Winston "crossed the floor" to join the Liberal Party. This was a dramatic step that was to pay dividends three years later when the Liberals defeated the Conservatives in a landslide. Winston was quickly given his first ministerial post of Under-Secretary of State for the Colonies.

In this year—1906—of the Liberal victory at the polls, Winston's book about his father, *Lord Randolph Churchill*, was published. It ranks, even today, as one of the outstanding biographies ever written of a father by a son.

In 1908, the year William H. Taft was elected President of the United States, Churchill was defeated in a by-election at Manchester Northwest after having been appointed president of the Board of Trade. On the very evening of his defeat in Manchester, however, he was invited to run as a candidate from Dundee, in Scotland, where he won by an overwhelming margin.

On September 12, 1908, Winston took one of the most important steps of his life. He took as his bride the lovely Miss Clementine Hozier, daughter of Colonel and Lady Blanche Hozier of Dundee. The wedding, at St. Margaret's in London, was one of the social events of the year. Despite the opinions of some that the marriage would not last, it was to become one of the happiest and most-enduring romances of the century. As Winston put it; "I married and lived happily ever afterwards."

Following a honeymoon in Italy, the couple settled down in a modest home near London's Queen Anne's Gate.

The years passed swiftly for the energetic Winston and his lovely bride.

In 1909 their first child was born, a daughter they named Diana. In 1910, Winston was appointed Home Secretary, which led to his being involved in the so-called "Sidney Street Affair." In his new office Winston was responsible for law and order in the country. When some gunmen who had slain three policemen were cornered in a house on Sidney Street, Winston promptly arrived to take charge. In his top hat and fancy coat, he looked quite out of place as bullets whizzed back and forth between the criminals and policemen. Eventually, the house caught fire and the criminals were burned to death. Churchill was criticized for becoming personally involved, but it was not to be the last time he would be so treated for leaving his desk and appearing at the scene of action.

In that same year—1911—Churchill was appointed First Lord of the Admiralty, which is roughly equivalent to the American Secretary of the Navy. With his appointment came a specific mandate to prepare the fleet for instant and constant readiness in case of war with Germany. Winston accepted the challenge with his usual zeal and energy. Recognizing his own lack of experience in naval matters, he promptly enlisted the aid of an old Admiral, Lord Fisher. From 1904 to 1910, Fisher had served as First Sea Lord—the equivalent of the American Chief of Naval Operations. He had revolutionized the British fleet and is generally regarded as the father of the modern battleship and modern navy.

In 1910, Churchill was appointed Home Secretary, which led to his being involved in the so-called "Sidney Street Affair." When some gunmen who had slain three policemen were cornered in a house on Sidney Street, Winston promptly arrived to take charge (right). In top hat and fancy coat, he looked quite out of place as bullets whizzed back and forth between the criminals and policemen.

L.C.T.

In his eagerness to learn as much about navy life as possible, Winston spent as much time as he could spare with the fleet. In the ensuing months he spent many days aboard various ships, from submarines to battleships and destroyers. Meanwhile, Clemmie, as he fondly called his wife, presented him with a son who, of course, could be given no other name than Randolph.

In his determination to insure the British navy's superiority over the German fleet, Winston pushed through many new ideas and reforms. One of his pet projects was the concept of a division of fast battleships that could outdistance any comparable ships in the world. Another major step taken by Churchill was the outfitting of five new battleships with untested 15-inch guns instead of the usual 13.5-inchers. Despite a hue and cry which rose throughout the navy and the nation, Winnie (as he was now popularly called) pushed ahead with the big guns. If they failed, the battleships would be useless. If they proved sound it could mean the margin of victory. Once again a Churchill "hunch" paid off. When war came in the summer of 1914, Winston's battleships could outshoot every ship in the German fleet.

From 1911 to 1915, Winston was instrumental in the creation of the Royal Naval Flying Corps. While other minds were convinced that the airplane would never be more than an expensive, untrustworthy toy, Winston began to explore the possibilities of the plane as a

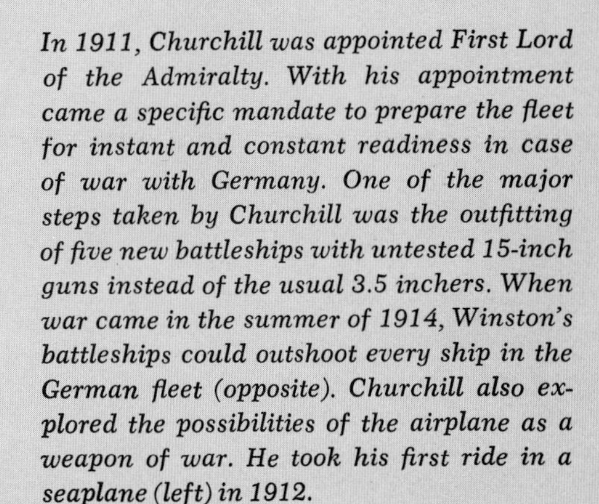

In 1911, Churchill was appointed First Lord of the Admiralty. With his appointment came a specific mandate to prepare the fleet for instant and constant readiness in case of war with Germany. One of the major steps taken by Churchill was the outfitting of five new battleships with untested 15-inch guns instead of the usual 3.5 inchers. When war came in the summer of 1914, Winston's battleships could outshoot every ship in the German fleet (opposite). Churchill also explored the possibilities of the airplane as a weapon of war. He took his first ride in a seaplane (left) in 1912.

weapon of war. He took his first ride in a seaplane in 1912, and though he admitted to some apprehension before the flight, he was soon won over completely to this new field of aviation.

Another example of Churchill's farsightedness regarding weapons of war was the tank, which he called a "landship." Until their use was proven, these machines were called "Winston's Folly" by less-imaginative people.

During that summer of 1914, when war clouds slowly gathered over Europe, Winston decided not to hold the usual summer naval maneuvers. Instead he ordered a test mobilization of the naval reserve fleets. This was in July, as the European crisis deepened following the assassination of Austrian Archduke Ferdinand at Sarajevo in Bosnia. As conditions worsened, Churchill next ordered that the reserves not be dispersed to their homes following the naval review which climaxed the summer mobilization activities. Finally, in the last week of peace, he ordered the fleet dispatched to their war stations and then, without legal authority or royal proclamation, sent out orders for a full mobilization. Three days later, on August 4, after Germany rejected an ultimatum, Britain declared war. Thanks to Churchill, the British fleet was manned and ready at their war stations. From his office in the Admiralty, Winston sent out this message to all his ships: "Commence hostilities against Germany."

The first task that fell to the British navy was to transport the army to the continent and, of course, to safeguard their passage. Meanwhile, the German army was pushing rapidly through Belgium and threatened to seize the chan-

nel ports. Much of Belgium had already fallen by the first of October but remnants of their army were still holding out near the great port of Antwerp. Though there were no British troops immediately at hand to send in relief, 8000 men of the Royal Naval Division were immediately dispatched and Churchill was sent to take charge of the expedition.

As it turned out, this stop-gap measure was too little and too late. But for five crucial days Antwerp held out against tremendous odds. Meanwhile the Allies were able to reach and fortify Ypres, Nieuport, and Dunkirk and save their northern flank from complete collapse. It was one of Winston's major successes of his career, though—due principally to the heavy British losses incurred—his efforts were not appreciated at the time.

On October 31, 1914, Turkey declared war on the side of Germany. In January of the following year, an appeal came from Russia, who in alliance with England was fighting the Turks, to make some sort of military demonstration against Turkey to relieve pressure on the Russian front. Churchill soon conceived a plan to force the Strait of Dardanelles which controls the ap-

A major example of Churchill's farsightedness regarding weapons of war was the tank, which he called a "landship." Until their use was proven, as in the battle illustrated below, these machines were called "Winston's Folly" by less-imaginative people. In August, 1914, after Germany rejected an ultimatum, Britain declared war. Thanks to Churchill, Britain was ready.

proaches to the Black Sea from the Mediterranean. If the strait could be forced, the wavering Balkan states might be induced to side with the Allies and also a helping hand could be extended through the Black Sea to Russia.

The action began on February 19, 1915, with the capture of the island of Lemnos. A month later a naval force under Admiral de Robeck tried to force the Narrows but gave up after four ships were sunk by mines. On April 25, major Allied landings were made on the Gallipoli peninsula but ill luck and incompetence of those commanders on the scene resulted in failure. In the meantime, Lord Fisher, who had never supported the Dardanelles scheme, resigned as First Sea Lord. Winston found himself the scapegoat for the debacle.

At home, a general dissatisfaction with the conduct of the war had forced Liberal Prime Minister Asquith to form a Coalition government with the Conservatives. Now both the Liberals and the Tories would have a say in the management of the war effort. The Conservatives, of course, looked upon Churchill as a traitor for having "crossed the floor" back in 1903. Now was their chance for revenge. Accordingly, before they would join the Liberals, they insisted that Churchill give up his post as First Lord of the Admiralty. He was to be placated by being made Chancellor of the Duchy of Lancaster.

In May, Winston resigned from his Admiralty post. This was, through all the ups and downs of his political fortunes, the lowest point of his career. Time, history, and an official commission would, however, eventually exonerate Winston of sole blame for the failure at Gallipoli.

In May, 1915, Churchill resigned from his Admiralty post, and in November he resigned from the cabinet. Once again battle called and he was soon in the uniform of a major in the Second Grenadier Guards (right). Within a month he had been promoted to lieutenant colonel and was given command of the Sixth Royal Scots Fusiliers.

Prophet of the Storm

The summer of 1915 was a period of ever-growing frustration for Winston Churchill. Though still a member of the cabinet and privy to the plans and strategy of the war, he had little influence in their making as Chancellor of the Duchy of Lancaster. At last he could stand it no longer, and in November he tendered his resignation from the cabinet. Once again battle called, and Winston was soon in the uniform of a major in the Second Grenadier Guards.

Within a month he had been promoted to lieutenant colonel and was placed in command of his own battalion—the Sixth Royal Scots Fusiliers. By now the war had become virtually a stalemate as millions of men manned the trenches on either side with neither able to make any headway. Churchill's battalion moved into the trenches at Ploegsteert Village, near Armentières, France, where it was to live in the hideous conditions of trench warfare but see little action. In the autumn of 1916, the now under-strength Fusiliers were absorbed into another battalion and, as the junior commander of the two units involved, Winston had to forfeit his command. About this time, many influential people at home were trying to convince him that a man of

By early 1916, the war had become virtually a stalemate as millions of men manned the trenches on either side with neither able to make any headway (below). The now under-strength Fusiliers were absorbed into another battalion that autumn, and as the junior commander of the two units involved, Winston had to forfeit his command. At last he resigned his commission and returned to England.

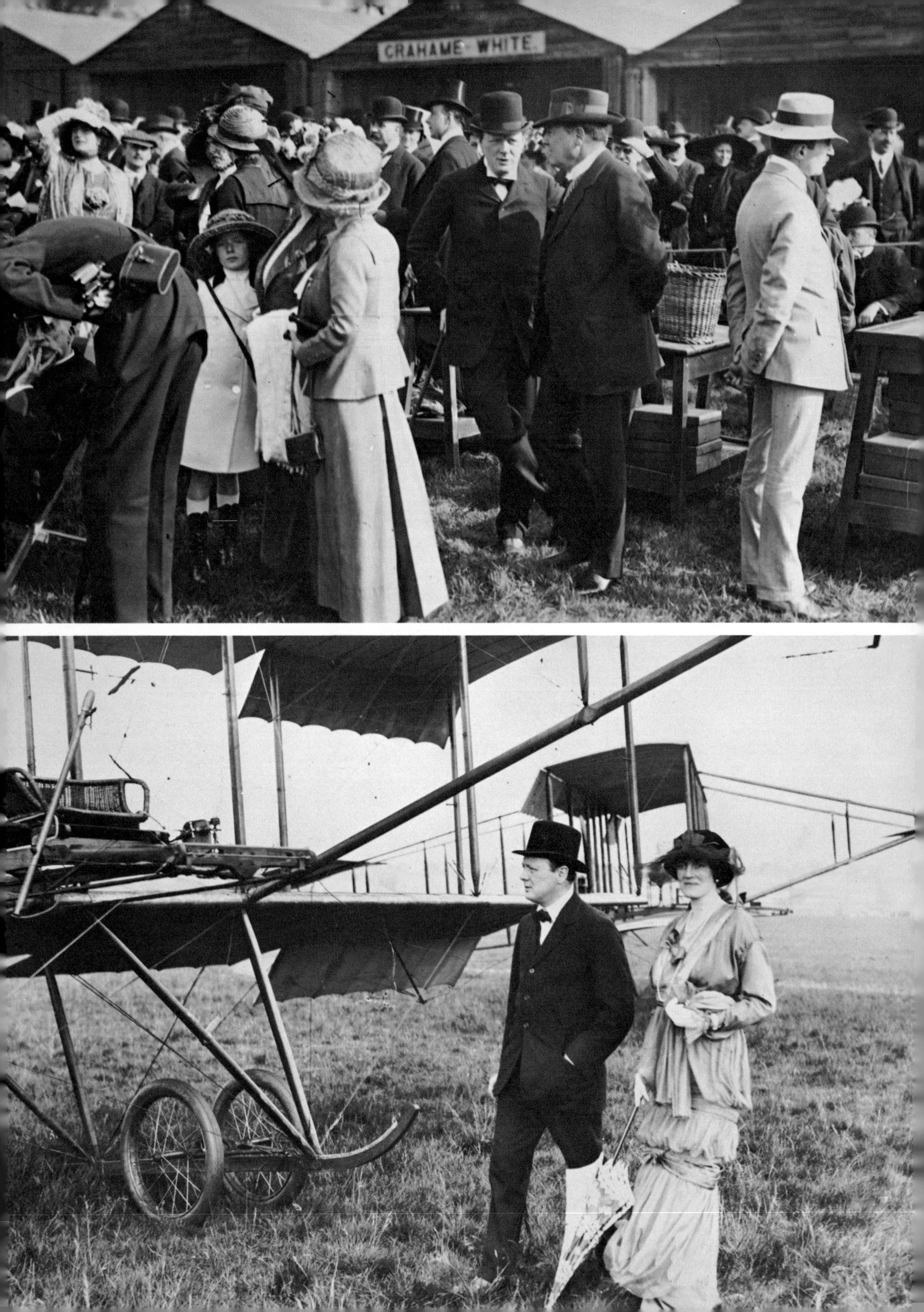
GRAHAME-WHITE.

his genius was wasting his time in a junior command in the trenches. At last Winston agreed, and he resigned his commission and returned to England.

In May of 1917, soon after the United States had entered the war, Prime Minister Lloyd George appointed Winston Minister of Munitions. In this capacity he was responsible for the production of guns, shells, armaments, and much of the other paraphernalia of war. He was also responsible for equipping the American armies as they arrived in France. For his efforts here, he was awarded the Distinguished Service Medal by the American commander, General John Pershing.

It was during his tenure as Minister of Munitions that Winston learned to fly. Unfortunately, his interest in aviation was not matched by his flying ability. In fact, it has been said that he was one of the very worst aviators of his day. All sorts of misfortunes befell him, but, amazingly, he escaped from each unscathed. Once his engine quit over the English Channel, but he was able to glide to a crash landing on the coast. He was equally unsuited as a navigator. Once he took off from an English airfield and headed for London under poor weather conditions. After a few hours of flight, the weather cleared, and Winston came fluttering back to earth—at an aerodrome in France! In the summer of 1919 he was involved in a spectacular crash at the airport in Croydon, near London. With the usual Churchill luck he emerged from the wreckage unhurt, but his passenger sustained severe injuries (he later recovered) and this decided Winston against piloting airplanes in the future.

With the Armistice on November 11, 1918, Winston's job as Minister of Munitions came to an end. In January of 1919, he was appointed Secretary of State for War and Air and found himself responsible for the demobilization of England's armed forces. His talents for organization were put to the test in this assignment, and under his leadership and direction more than three million men were processed back to civilian life in the first six months.

In May, 1917, Churchill was appointed Minister of Munitions. During his tenure in this post, his interest in aviation became very great. He is shown opposite, top, at an aviation rally, and opposite, bottom, visiting an airfield with Mrs. Churchill. He has been called one of the very worst aviators of his day, and all sorts of misfortunes befell him. Once his engine quit over the English Channel (above), but he was able to glide to a crash landing on the coast.

In 1921, Churchill was made Colonial Secretary, a position which at this point in history required an aggressive spirit and a fresh approach to problems. He negotiated a peace treaty with the leaders of the Irish Rebellion—the first really constructive step toward peace in Ireland. The result of the treaty was the establishment of the Irish Free State under its own government, and eventually a final settlement. In Iraq, he helped reach a peaceful solution with rebellious Arabs.

Winston's mother died in 1921. She had become increasingly close to her son as his political star had risen and, unlike Lord Randolph, had lived to see the great potential of her son. Her death was the second in Winston's family within a year. A daughter, Marigold Frances, born in 1918, had died only a short while before.

In 1922 the long-standing Coalition government fell from power, and Churchill once again stood for election at Dundee. A few days before the campaign began, however, he was stricken with appendicitis and rushed to a hospital for an operation. Though Clemmie and many loyal friends campaigned vigorously for the sick man, none could match his style or state his case as solidly as he might have done. He emerged from his sickbed just two days before the poll—too late to really get into the fight. The results were disastrous. He lost by over ten thousand votes. Despite the drubbing, he retained his sense of humor. "I now find myself," he said, "without an office, without a seat, without a party, and without an appendix."

For two years, Winston remained without a seat in the House, though on two more occasions he ran for election—and lost. The restless spirit of Winston Churchill could not readily accept inactivity, and he set about keeping himself busy. He had tried painting as a hobby back in 1915, and now in 1922 he returned once more to this fascinating pastime. He had a natural—even gifted—flair for painting. He painted just for fun, but exhibited some of his paintings under the names "Charles Morin" or "Mr. Winter." These were quickly purchased. One of his paintings of the 1920's was sold for charity at a price of 1310 pounds (roughly $6500). He also took up bricklaying as a pastime and helped build a cottage at Chartwell Manor, his country estate in Kent.

In September of 1922, another daughter, Mary, was added to the Churchill clan. It was a happy family caught up in the excitement and whirl of activity generated by their effervescent father. Clemmie was an excellent and devoted wife and mother who geared the family life to Winston's important work.

In 1924, fortune smiled once again on Winston Churchill. By now he had found he could no longer support the Liberal cause, which was becoming more and more associated with socialism. Accordingly, he stood for election as a Constitutionalist in the rural constituency of Epping, winning by a wide margin. In this same election, the Conservatives were returned to power and the new Prime Minister, Stanley Baldwin, offered Winston the position of Chancellor of the Exchequer. Once more Churchill was back in the Conservative fold, which he had deserted back in 1904.

Winston's tenure as Chancellor of the Exchequer was destined to be one of the least-distinguished periods of his life. It

All during his lifetime, Winston Churchill had a boundless energy and found time to take part in outdoor pastimes such as pheasant shooting (opposite top), boar hunting (opposite, left bottom), and playing polo (opposite, right bottom), which he continued playing until he was more than fifty years old.

was during this period that a general strike severely crippled the nation's economy. Churchill's fear of socialism led him to actions that caused him to become very unpopular with the workingmen, who were striking for better wages. In 1929 the Baldwin government lost a general election, and though Winston was re-elected, he was out of office once again. Years later he would say, "Everybody said I was the worst Chancellor of the Exchequer that ever was. And now I'm inclined to agree with them."

The period from 1929 to 1939 was spent in a "political wilderness." It was a productive period for Winston in the literary field, however. During this time he wrote many books, including *My Early Life*, which was published in 1930; *Thoughts and Adventures* in 1932; and *Great Contemporaries* in 1937. His much-acclaimed four-volume work called *Marlborough, His Life and Times* was done during the period from 1932 to 1938. In 1931 Churchill traveled to America on a lecture tour.

Back in England, Churchill grew increasingly concerned over the rearming of Germany and the rise of the Nazi party under Adolf Hitler. He began to voice warnings about where this would eventually lead. His was to be a nearly solitary voice crying to an unheeding nation to prepare and arm itself. The English people, who had seen the flower of a generation trammeled in the trenches of France, could not believe that any people would ever want to wage war again.

As early as November of 1933, Churchill told the House of Commons, "a philosophy of blood-lust is being inculcated into their (German) youth . . . this is the same mighty Germany which once fought all the world and almost beat the world . . . ." His warnings fell on deaf ears.

Churchill was especially concerned about the growing might of the German air force, or *Luftwaffe*. To the House, in February of 1934, he said, "This cursed, hellish invention and development of war from the air has revolutionized our position. We are not the same kind of country we used to be when we were an island, only twenty years ago."

On March 7, 1936, Hitler's armies occupied the Rhineland demilitarized zone in violation of the Versailles Treaty. Neither France nor England nor the League of Nations would risk war to throw Hitler out. Hitler had gained in prestige while the League of Nations lost the faith of the world.

A brief interlude in the gathering storm appeared when Winston was called in to be adviser to King Edward VIII who planned to abdicate his throne in order to marry an American divorcée. Edward's mind was made up, however, and Churchill, after announcing his support of the King's plan, helped him write his abdication speech. Edward's brother, the Duke of York, became King George VI.

On March 11, 1938, Hitler invaded Austria. Again no action was taken by other European countries. Again Churchill arose in the House of Commons with a warning: "There is only one choice open, not only to us, but to other countries, either to submit like Austria, or else take effective measures to ward off the danger, and if it cannot be warded off to cope with it. . . . Where are we going to be two years hence? . . ."

The English were not alone in their blindness. France and the other countries of Europe could not, or would not, believe that the fanatic little ex-corporal in Berlin meant them any harm. After each conquest, Hitler would say: "This is all I want. Germany's demands are now satisfied." And peace-loving people everywhere believed him. Across

Churchill took up bricklaying as a hobby and helped build a cottage (opposite bottom) at Chartwell Manor (opposite top), his country estate in Kent.

As early as November of 1933, Churchill was becoming increasingly concerned over the rearming of Germany and the rise of the Nazi party under Adolf Hitler. In 1936, Hitler's armies occupied the Rhineland demilitarized zone in violation of the Versailles Treaty. In March of 1938, Hitler invaded Austria. His next demands were for Sudetenland, a very large portion of Czechoslovakia. German troops are shown at left entering the town of Reichenberg, which was by then a German town in Sudetenland.

". . . . All is over. Silent, mournful, abandoned, broken, Czechoslovakia recedes into the darkness . . . ."

the Atlantic, Americans watched impassively as the Nazi appetite fed on the disunited nations of Europe.

Hitler's next demands were for the Sudetenland—a very large portion of Czechoslovakia. Neville Chamberlain, now Prime Minister, made several trips to Germany to confer with Hitler. After first returning from Berchtesgaden with Hitler's demands, to which the Czechs reluctantly agreed in the name of peace, Chamberlain soon discovered that Hitler had upped his price. The Prime Minister balked and Hitler sent an ultimatum giving five days to meet his demands.

While negotiations were going on, Churchill made a statement to the public: "The partition of Czechoslovakia . . . amounts to the complete surrender of the Western Democracies to the Nazi threat of force. Such a collapse will bring peace or security neither to England nor France. . . . It is not Czechoslovakia alone which is menaced, but also the freedom and democracy of all nations."

Once more Chamberlain flew off to visit with Hitler, who had declared: "This is the last territorial claim I have to make in Europe." The scene this time was Munich, the lovely old Bavarian city whose name was to become synonymous with "appeasement." Once more, all of Hitler's demands were met, and Chamberlain flew back to London talking about peace with honor.

To Churchill it was anything but an honorable settlement. To the House of Commons he said: "All is over. Silent, mournful, abandoned, broken, Czechoslovakia recedes into the darkness. . . . And do not suppose that this is the end. This is only the beginning of the reckoning. This is only the first sip, the first foretaste of a bitter cup which will be proffered to us year by year unless, by a supreme recovery of moral health and martial vigor, we arise again and take our stand for freedom as in the olden time."

How sadly true these words would prove to be. Too late, Britain awoke to the fact that Churchill had been right all along. In March of 1939, Hitler took over all of Czechoslovakia and soon was making demands of Poland. Churchill's unheeded warnings of the past decade came echoing back with each new Nazi threat or conquest.

When in the waning summer of 1939 Hitler released his armies against Poland, the British nation turned in anxiety to the man who had foretold these tragic events. Within a few months, they would place their fate in his hands. The years of preparation were about to reach their climax as Winston Churchill at last met his moment of destiny.

We Shall Never Give In

"Winston is back."

So read the happy signal to the British fleet announcing Churchill's appointment to his old World War I post as First Lord of the Admiralty. Churchill accepted the position only a few hours after the declaration of war on September 3, 1939. Prime Minister Chamberlain offered him a seat in the War Cabinet as well, giving Winston a voice in making government policies.

"Once again defense of the rights of a weak state, outraged and invaded by unprovoked aggression, forced us to draw the sword," Winston would later write. "Once again we must fight for life and honour against all the might and fury of the valiant, disciplined, and ruthless German race. Once again! So be it."

Within three weeks Poland had fallen. For Winston Churchill and the British navy, the war began in earnest almost immediately. At nine o'clock on the evening war was declared, the passenger liner *Athenia,* outbound from England, was torpedoed and sunk with the loss of 112 lives—28 of them American. The German U-boat war had started.

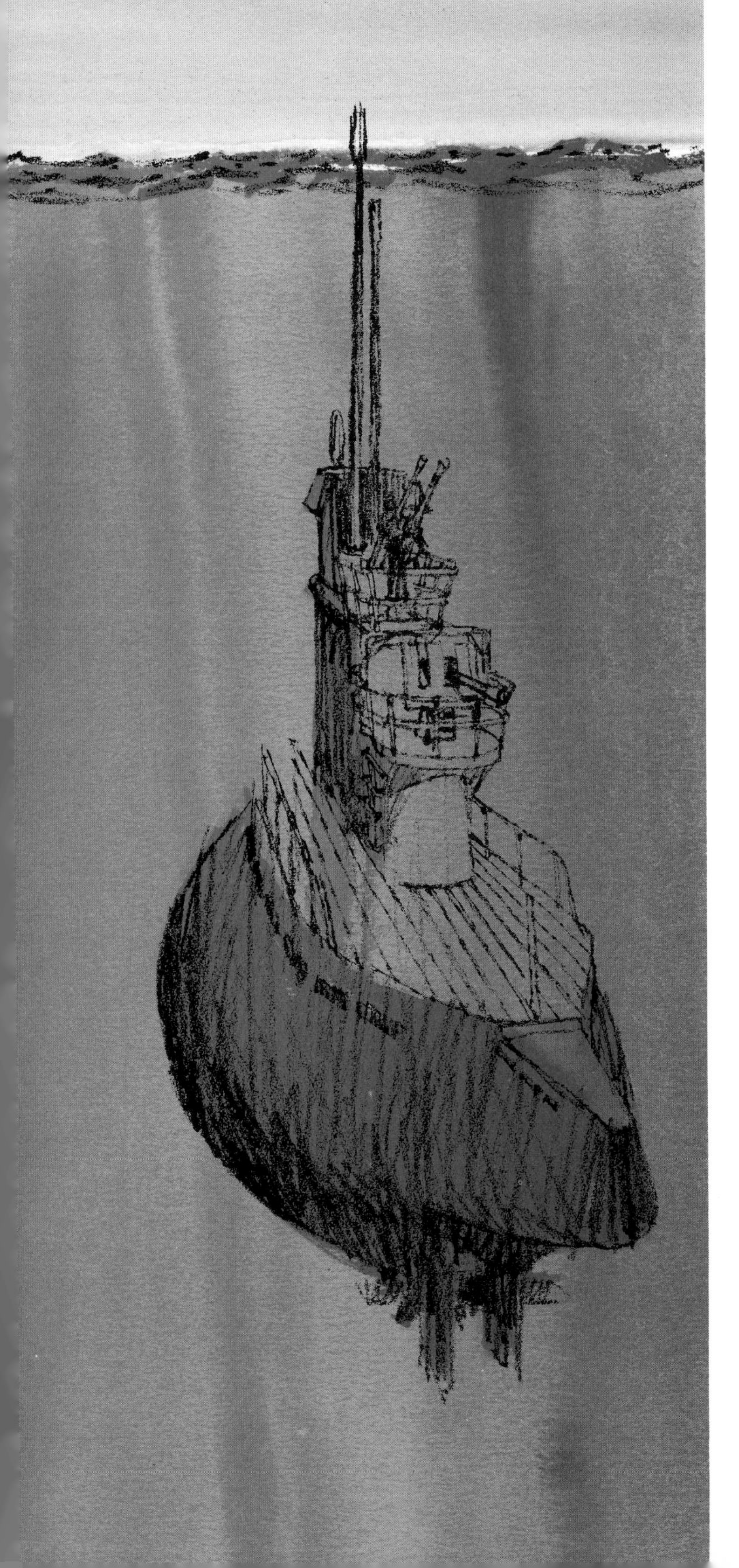

When Britain declared war on Germany, Churchill was again appointed First Lord of the Admiralty. In order to reduce the German U-boat threat and keep the sea lanes open to the British Isles, he began a building program of destroyers and other sub-killers, and employed the convoy method of herding groups of ships across the open seas (below), along with a system of evasive routing.

This marked the beginning of a very grave threat. The British Isles had to import a great percentage of their food and materials from all parts of the vast British Empire—Canada, Australia, India, South Africa, and many other distant places. As First Lord of the Admiralty, it fell to Churchill to find some means of reducing the U-boat threat and to keep open the sea lanes—the lifelines of the British Isles.

Winston attacked the problem from many sides. A frantic effort was made to equip as many ships as possible with "Asdics"—devices for detecting submarines. A top-priority building program of destroyers and other sub-killers was initiated. The convoy method of herding groups of ships across the open seas was put into use, along with a system of evasive routing. German U-boats lurked beneath the surface along all the established water routes, and these traps had to be avoided whereever possible. The submarine threat would continue to be one of tremendous proportions for many, many months to come.

The bitter debate that began on May 7, 1940, in the House of Commons demonstrated the lack of confidence most Britons now felt in Prime Minister Chamberlain. Very soon thereafter, Neville Chamberlain stepped down from the leadership of the British nation, and Winston Churchill was called to see the King. His walk with destiny began.

"In my long political experience," Churchill wrote later, "I had held most of the great offices of State, but I readily admit that the post which had now fallen to me was the one I liked best. Power, for the sake of lording it over fellow creatures or adding to personal pomp, is rightly judged base. But power in a national crisis, when a man believes he knows what orders should be given, is a blessing."

On May 15, 1940, Churchill sent his first message to President Roosevelt as Prime Minister. In it he asked for the loan of forty or fifty old American destroyers, which were vitally needed to keep open the sea lifelines to the British Isles. There were other things the British would need, including aircraft, munitions, and anti-aircraft weapons. Now that he was Prime Minister, Winston signed the letter "Former Naval Person."

Mr. Roosevelt replied that he would "facilitate to the utmost the Allied Governments obtaining the latest types of United States aircraft equipment, ammunition, and steel."

On the continent, the powerful Nazi attack on Belgium, Holland, Luxembourg, and France continued unchecked. The Germans had swept, in a giant arc, around the massive defenses of the Maginot Line. Holland, unprepared and hopelessly overpowered, fell in just four days. Queen Wilhelmina and the Dutch government escaped to London. King Leopold III of Belgium capitulated on May 26, an act that exposed the flanks of the British Expeditionary Force and much of the French army. These armies were cut off and driven, with their backs to the sea, to ports along the English Channel. It seemed as if they were soon to be gobbled up by the onrushing German *Wehrmacht*.

On May 10, 1940, Neville Chamberlain resigned as Prime Minister and Winston Churchill was asked to form a new government. The photograph at right was taken of the new Prime Minister by Mr. Cecil Beaton.

As thousands upon thousands of British and French soldiers crouched among the sand dunes of the beaches of Dunkirk, a wave of apprehension passed through the British people. It was a fear, Churchill reported, "not of death or wounds or material loss, but of defeat and the final ruin of Britain."

The admiralty signaled for the start of "Operation Dynamo," a chapter in history that Winston has called "The Deliverance of Dunkerque." Every type of craft, large or small, that could reach the scene was pressed into service to make shuttle runs across the narrow, but often treacherous, English Channel. As the valiant men of the Royal Air Force struggled vainly to ward off waves of German bombers overhead, the soldiers waded out to waiting boats. The Germans smashed with all their might at the desperate few who fought a rearguard action to defend the dwindling perimeter. But the bulk of the army got away. By June 4, some 338,000 British and Allied troops had landed in England. The few remaining in the now-tiny defense perimeter surrendered at last to the angry and frustrated Germans. The evacuation of Dunkirk was over.

Two weeks later, France sued for peace and Hitler insisted that the surrender be held in a railroad dining car in the Forest of Compiègne, where Marshal Foch had dictated armistice terms to the Germans in 1918. The terms were signed on June 22. Britain now stood alone.

Later, Churchill tried to raise the spirits of the stricken nation. "Frenchmen!" he cried, "re-arm your spirits.... Never will I believe the soul of France is dead! Never will I believe that her place amongst the greatest nations of the world has been lost forever! . . . The story is not yet finished . . . have hope and faith and all will come right."

He reminded them, too, of British determination. ". . . We shall never stop, never weary, and never give in..."

He closed with a prophecy. "Good night then," he said. "Sleep to gather strength for the morning. For the morning will come. Brightly will it shine on the brave and true, kindly upon all who suffer for the cause, gloriously upon the tombs of heroes. Thus will shine the dawn. *Vive la France!*"

During this terrible, fateful month of June, 1940, the words of Winston Churchill rang out in eloquent expression of the feelings of the British people.

On June 4 he said, ". . . we shall not flag or fail. We shall go on to the end, we shall fight in France, we shall fight in the seas and oceans, we shall fight with growing confidence and growing strength in the air, we shall defend our island, whatever the cost may be, we shall fight on the beaches, we shall fight on the landing grounds, we shall fight in the fields and in the streets, we shall fight in the hills; we shall never surrender. . . ."

With the fall of France, he spoke again on June 18. ". . . the Battle of France is over. I expect the Battle of Britain is about to begin. Upon this battle depends the survival of Christian civilization . . . our own British life . . . and our Empire. Hitler knows he will have to break us in this island or lose the war. If we fail, then the whole world, including the United States . . . will sink into the abyss of a new Dark Age. . . ."

He ended with a phrase that will ring through history for as long as men stand and fight for an honorable cause.

"Let us therefore brace ourselves to our duties, and so bear ourselves that, if the British Empire and its Commonwealth last for a thousand years, men will still say:

"This was their finest hour!"

The powerful Nazi attack on the Low Countries and France began on May 10, 1940. Holland fell in just four days; Belgium capitulated on May 26; France surrendered on June 22, and Hitler insisted that the papers be signed in a railroad dining car in the Forest of Compiègne (opposite), where Marshal Foch dictated armistice terms to the Germans in 1918.

2418 D

The Battle of Britain

The summer months of 1940 were the most desperate in British history. All of Britain's allies now lay beneath the boot of Nazi tyranny. The British Isles lay virtually unarmed with most of their tanks, field guns, and transport now in the hands of the Germans on the beaches of Dunkirk.

Across the sea, Americans watched the events in Europe with growing alarm. It was apparent to most that if Britain fell, war would soon come to America. Much to Churchill's pleasure, the American War Department released surplus or outdated stocks of arms, munitions, and aircraft to Great Britain. More than forty-three million dollars' worth arrived in Britain during the critical month of June.

These anxious summer months were ones of frantic preparation in England. The powerful German army now lay only a few miles across the waters of the English Channel. Invasion could come at any day, at any hour. Time was of the essence and Churchill rallied his countrymen to great efforts.

He now turned his full energies to readying his "island" for the German invasion, which could come at any moment. Though he was sixty-seven years old, Churchill became a veritable dynamo of energy. He seemed to be everywhere. Men who were constructing defenses on the North Sea and Channel coasts were happily surprised at the sight of his robust figure inspecting their work. Military units of all the services were visited as Churchill went to see for himself the state of their readiness and morale.

It would have been impossible for most men to bear up under such a strain for a long period of time. Winston did it, however, and he has written of his special method that "greatly extended my daily capacity for work."

"I always went to bed for at least one hour as early as possible in the afternoon and exploited to the full my happy gift of falling almost immediately into deep sleep. By this means I was able to press a day and a half's work into one."

During the summer months of 1940, Churchill turned his full energies to readying England for the German invasion, which could come at any moment. He became a veritible dynamo of energy and seemed to be everywhere. Military units of all the services were visited as Churchill went to see for himself the state of their readiness and morale. Opposite, he stands under the guns of the cruiser Exeter.

The Battle of Britain began on July 10, with the launching of heavy raids against the ports along England's southern coast. The Germans hoped to lure the R.A.F. into combat and gradually wear them down with overwhelming numbers. In August the raids shifted to the British airfields, radar installations, and "sector stations," which coordinated the fighter defenses. This was the most critical phase of the battle.

Hitler now hoped to coax the British to surrender by mercilessly pounding London to rubble. Beginning on September 7, and for fifty-seven consecutive nights, an average of 200 German bombers attacked the city. While the civilian population huddled in bomb shelters or in subways, searchlights streaked across the London skies as a thunderous barrage of anti-aircraft guns mingled with the crash of exploding bombs.

The German aim, Churchill said, "was to break the spirit of the Londoner. . . . I felt a deep sense of the strain and suffering that was being borne throughout the world's largest capital city. How long would it go on? How much more would they have to bear? What were the limits of their vitality?"

Churchill made frequent visits to the areas most severely struck and the people always demonstrated their confidence in him with rousing cheers. On more than one occasion Winston was reduced to tears. "You see," the people said, "he really cares. He's crying."

"They were tears not of sorrow," Churchill remembered, "but of wonder and admiration." Splendid virtues were displayed, he said, "by millions of ordinary humble people, who proved to

---

The Battle of Britain began on July 10, 1940, with the launching of heavy raids against the ports along England's southern coast. Later, Hitler hoped to coax the British to surrender by mercilessly pounding London to rubble. Beginning on September 7, and for fifty-seven consecutive nights, an average of 200 German bombers attacked the city. In the photograph at right, a German bomber wings over London.

the world the strength of a community nursed in freedom. . . . At this time anyone would have been proud to be a Londoner."

In November of that fateful 1940, the Germans once more shifted their attacks—this time to other cities, although London still remained the main target. On the fourteenth of that month, the historic old city of Coventry was struck with a series of raids that lasted from dusk until dawn. Four hundred persons died that night and several thousand were injured. Later, other cities were mauled in the same manner —Plymouth, Manchester, Liverpool, and Glasgow, among others. But, as Churchill would write later, "It did not matter where the blow struck, the nation was as sound as the sea is salt."

Gradually the *Blitz* of London decreased to sporadic attacks. The Battle of Britain was won by the unconquerable spirit of the British people and their determined leader and by the courage, skill, and tenacity of the R.A.F. Churchill paid special tribute to the fighter pilots in a speech in the House of Commons. "Never in the field of human conflict was so much owed by so many to so few."

As the fight for life was being carried on in the skies over England, other battles were being waged in other parts of the world. On the high seas, the war against the U-boats was growing in intensity as the Germans proclaimed a total blockade of the British Isles. The powerful German battleship *Bismarck* broke out into the Atlantic and sank H.M.S. *Hood,* the pride of the British fleet, but was herself sunk three days later in one of the epic sea battles of history.

Meanwhile, the gallant saga of courage and bravery of the British people had stirred the hearts of Americans. Tales of Nazi barbarity in the occupied countries were also beginning to reach American ears. Gradually, the country became less neutral in its attitude toward the war.

In early 1941, the United States Congress passed what Churchill called "the most unsordid act in the history of any nation." It was called Lend-Lease. Under this program the President was allowed to furnish supplies to any nation whose defense was deemed vital to the security of the United States. All the goods, from ships and airplanes to food and tanks, were loaned or leased. This meant that the British, whose dollar reserves had by now all been spent, could continue to order and receive any and all goods they required to fight the war. America had indeed become the "arsenal of Democracy."

Meanwhile, the battles on the deserts of Libya and Egypt see-sawed back and forth as first one side and then the other held the upper hand. In April of 1941, the Germans joined with the Italians in invading Greece and Yugoslavia. By May, the Axis held most of the Mediterranean except Malta, Gibraltar, and Egypt.

In June of that year, Hitler invaded Russia. England no longer stood alone. A longtime foe of communism, Churchill nonetheless welcomed the Russians as allies. "Any man or state who fights on

As the fight for life was being carried on in the skies over England, other battles were being waged in other parts of the world. On the high seas, the war against the U-boats was growing in intensity as the Germans proclaimed a total blockade of the British Isles. The powerful German battleship Bismarck *broke out into the Atlantic and sank* H.M.S. Hood, *the pride of the British fleet, but was herself sunk three days later in one of the epic sea battles of history (above).*

against Nazidom will have our aid," he said. "Any man or state who marches with Hitler is our foe."

On August 9, 1941, two great warships sailed into Placentia Bay in Newfoundland. On one, the U.S.S. *Augusta,* was the President of the United States. On the other, the H.M.S. *Prince of Wales,* was Prime Minister Winston Churchill. This was to be the first of several wartime meetings between the two great leaders of the free world.

Out of this historic meeting came a document known as the Atlantic Charter. It was a joint Anglo-American declaration of peace aims. Among other things, the charter expressed the right of nations to choose their form of government and to live in a world free from want and fear. It condemned aggression and sought to promote friendly collaboration among the peoples of the world. It called on all nations to give up the use of force and disarm.

Of the meeting with Roosevelt, Churchill reported, "I am sure I have established warm and deep personal relations with our great friend."

The next meeting of the two leaders would come only a little more than four months later, this time in Washington, D.C., on the twenty-second of December. At this second meeting the two were more than just warm friends. They were comrades in arms. Two weeks earlier, on December 7, 1941, the Japanese had attacked Pearl Harbor. The United States, too, was now at war. The combination, which Churchill called "The Grand Alliance," was now a reality.

"No American will think it wrong of me if I proclaim that to have the United States at our side was to me the greatest joy," Churchill wrote later. When the news first arrived of the Japanese attack on Pearl Harbor, Winston immediately put through a call to President Roosevelt, who confirmed the report.

"We all are in the same boat now," Mr. Roosevelt said.

For Winston, America's entry into the war meant the assurance of final victory. He knew that for the first few months defeats were still to be expected. But he had faith in the industrial might of America. He foresaw, too, the tremendous military strength which the fully aroused United States could muster. Victory was now only a matter of time and sacrifice.

Three weeks after the Pearl Harbor disaster, Churchill arrived in Washington, D.C., for a meeting with President Roosevelt. On the day after Christmas, the Prime Minister spoke to Congress, whose members gave him a warm welcome.

On December 30, he spoke to the Canadian Parliament and reminded them of how the French generals had predicted that "In three weeks England will have her neck wrung like a chicken." "Some chicken!" Churchill exclaimed, "Some neck!" The Canadians roared with delight.

Out of the meeting in Washington came an agreement as to the fundamental joint strategy that the Allies would pursue in the coming months and years. Basically, this recognized Churchill's policy of defeating Germany first, after which they would concentrate their efforts toward the defeat of Japan.

Throughout the first half of 1942, the Allied fortunes of war continued to dip. The Japanese advance raced almost unchecked in the Pacific and Indian Ocean areas. The Germans were virtually at the gates of Moscow, and Rommel—the "Desert Fox"—was pushing the British back in Libya. U-boats continued taking a heavy toll of Allied shipping in the Atlantic.

Throughout the first half of 1942, the Allied fortunes of war continued to dip. The Japanese advance raced almost unchecked in the Pacific and Indian Ocean areas. The Germans were virtually at the gates of Moscow, and Rommel, the "Desert Fox," was pushing the British back in Libya. U-boats continued taking a heavy toll of Allied shipping in the Atlantic. In August of 1942, Churchill visited the Middle East. He is shown, opposite, in the Alamein area. Two months later, General Montgomery launched an attack at El Alamein against Rommel's Afrika Korps. *By the first week in November, the Germans were in full retreat. To Churchill this marked ". . . the turning of the Hinge of Fate. . . . before Alamein we never had a victory. After Alamein we never had a defeat."*

Then, in October of 1942, General Montgomery launched an attack at El Alamein against Rommel's *Afrika Korps*. By the first week of November, the Germans were in full retreat. To Churchill this marked "... the turning of the Hinge of Fate. It may almost be said, 'before Alamein we never had a victory. After Alamein we never had a defeat.'"

On November 8, Operation "Torch" began with major American and British forces landing in Morocco and Algeria under the command of General Eisenhower. As Montgomery pushed from the east, Eisenhower's forces advanced from the west and the Germans were soon cornered in Tunisia. By May 13, 1943, all of North Africa lay in Allied hands.

Meanwhile, in January of 1943, President Roosevelt had met with Churchill at the now famous Casablanca Conference. The Free French leaders, Generals de Gaulle and Giraud, also attended the meeting. It was decided at this conference that the Allies would accept only "unconditional surrender" from their enemies.

Before leaving Morocco, Churchill and Roosevelt journeyed to Marrakech, the beautiful palm-ringed city that for centuries had been the terminus of camel caravan routes. For a few hours they put aside their cares and relaxed in the quiet beauty of this ancient land.

The two met again in Washington, D.C., in May of 1943 and, together with their top military advisers, set a date for the invasion of France, which would be called Operation "Overlord."

By mid-1943 the hinge of fate had fully turned. The great industrial might of America was sending forth the arms and supplies of war in tremendous volume. The ever-growing British, American, and Russian armies were beginning the squeeze that would inexorably snuff out the life of Hitler's Nazis and the Japanese warlords.

Churchill went to Washington again in September of 1943. Here a unique incident occurred when President Roosevelt went to his home at Hyde Park and left the White House in Winston's care to use as his headquarters. This act pointed up the close relationship between the two men and the two nations they represented.

In November of 1943, Churchill was off again on another jaunt, this time to Cairo for a meeting with Roosevelt and the Chinese leader, Chiang Kai-shek. From there Roosevelt and Churchill proceeded to Teheran, Iran, for an historic meeting with Russian Premier Joseph Stalin. Here the Allies announced they had completed plans for future operations against Germany.

At Carthage, on the way home from the meetings, Churchill suddenly came down with pneumonia. Ordered to bed by his doctors, he chafed at his immobility. His daughter Sarah, who had accompanied him, read aloud to keep him entertained. One morning, much to Winston's surprise, Sarah walked in with her mother. Clemmie had made the long and hazardous flight in an unheated plane to be at his side.

The patient and his entourage were subsequently removed to his favorite rest haven—Marrakech—where his remarkable recuperative powers seemed to do their best work. By mid-January of 1944 he was in top form once again and sailed home to England.

As the year 1944 neared its midpoint, the Allies were advancing steadily on every front throughout the world. In Italy they had cracked the formidable Gustav line and were advancing on Rome. The names Salerno, Anzio, and Cassino, little known a few months before, would now live forever in the history books.

By the middle of 1944, the Allies were advancing steadily on every front throughout the world. In Italy they had cracked the formidable Gustav line and were advancing on Rome. The names Salerno, Anzio, and Cassino, little known a few months before, would now live forever in the history books. The drawing at right shows an Allied artillery position. The camouflage net helped protect the position from detection by the enemy.

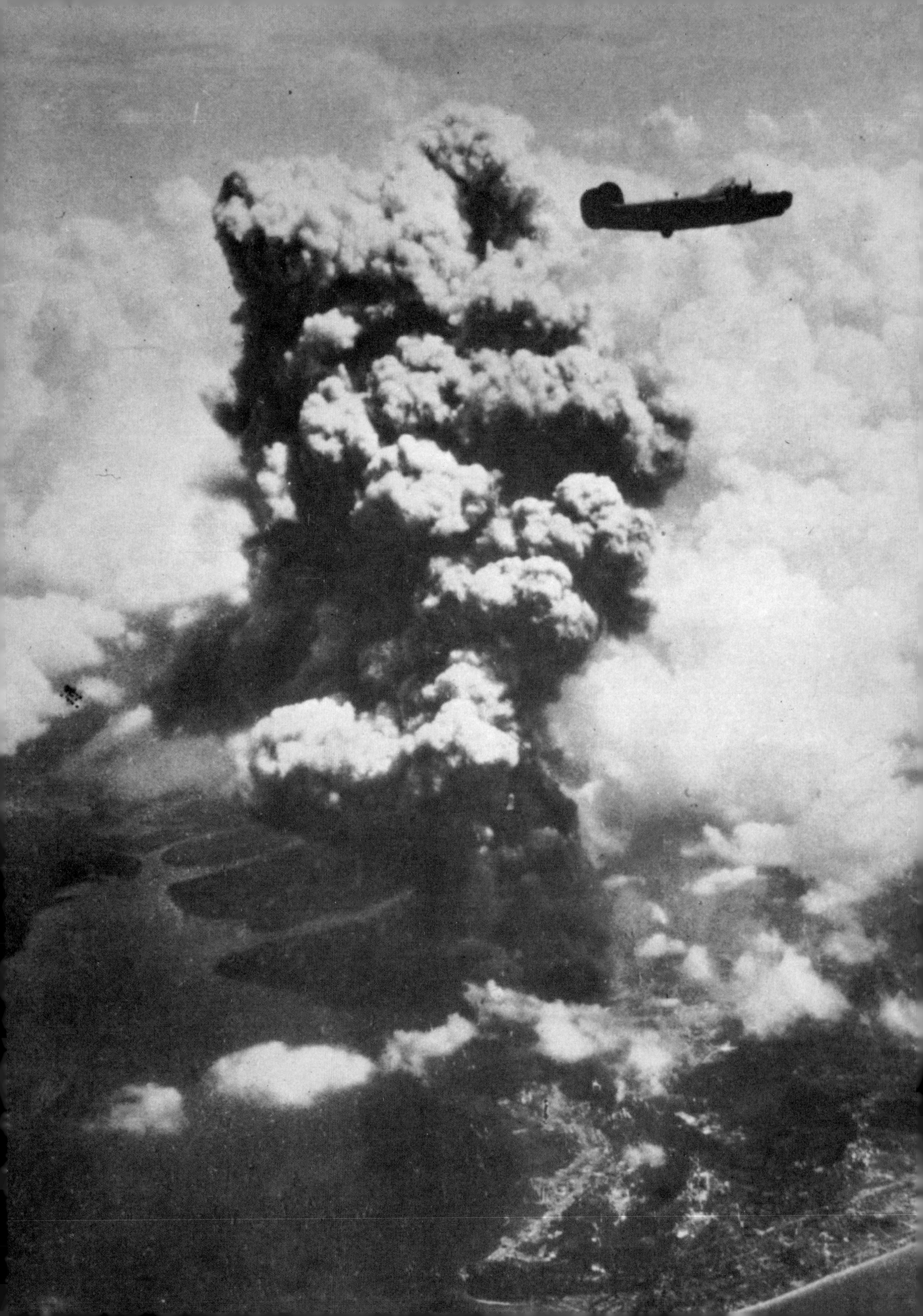

In the skies, the Allied air offensive was paying back, with terrible interest, the bombings of London during the *Blitz*.

In Russia, the Germans were suffering severe setbacks, and by June had been nearly pushed off Russian soil. In the Pacific, General MacArthur was leapfrogging his way back through the islands, which had fallen into Japanese hands two years before. Before the end of the year his promise to return to the Philippines would be fulfilled.

In the pre-dawn darkness of June 6, 1944, vast armadas of ships and landing craft moved silently across the English Channel to a rendezvous off the beaches of Normandy. These beaches had the secret code names of "Omaha," "Utah," "Gold," "Juno," and "Sword." Soon after daybreak a flash radio message went out around the world: "Under the command of General Eisenhower, Allied naval forces, supported by strong air forces, began landing Allied armies this morning on the coast of France."

By nightfall on that famous D-Day, some 150,000 Allied troops had landed on the soil of France. Churchill had wanted to be there, but King George and General Eisenhower managed to talk him out of it.

On June 10, however, Winston managed to get over to France, where he met with General Montgomery and toured the British area. On the way home on the destroyer *Kelvin,* Churchill asked the captain to approach the German-held area, where the ship fired several rounds at Nazi gun positions. Happily, the bigger German guns did not return the fire, but Winston's old war-horse spirit was at least somewhat satisfied.

In the skies, the Allied air offensive was paying back, with terrible interest, the bombings of London during the Blitz. *Allied aircraft are shown at left during an air raid over Germany.*

Exactly one week after D-Day, a new and even more terrifying ordeal than the *Blitz* fell upon London. On June 13, the first of the flying bombs, or "doodlebugs" as Londoners came to call them, exploded in a London suburb killing six people. These "buzz bombs" were pilotless jet aircraft that carried a ton of explosives.

Once again, as during the *Blitz*, the ingenuity and steadfast courage of the British people were to prevail. Special defenses were quickly set up to meet this new threat, and by the end of August the V-1 buzz bomb had been mastered.

Next, Hitler launched his most terrible weapon of all—the V-2 rocket. Though it carried only the same explosive load as the V-1, the new missile had a speed of some 4000 mph and was in the air only three or four minutes. Whereas one could hear the buzz bombs coming, the V-2 approached in silence. Once airborne, there was no defense against the rocket. The R.A.F., however, blasted with vigor at the rocket bases and kept the launchings to a minimum. The end to the V-2s came when British and Canadian armies overran the launching bases in Holland.

In August of 1944, Churchill went to Rome for a meeting with Tito, the Yugoslav guerrilla leader. A few weeks later, he was back across the Atlantic for the Second Quebec Conference with President Roosevelt, at which they discussed the postwar demarcation zones of Germany. A month later, Winston was back in Moscow for another conference with Stalin.

On Armistice Day, November 11, Churchill returned to Paris, which had been liberated on the twenty-eighth of August. In company with General de Gaulle, he placed a wreath upon the tomb of the Unknown Warrior at the Arc de Triomphe. Then Churchill and de Gaulle led a massive and joyous parade down the Champs Elysées.

In February of 1945 came the historic Yalta Conference on the Russian Crimean peninsula on the Black Sea. The three major participants were Churchill, Roosevelt, and Stalin. It was here that the convening of the United Nations Charter was announced.

While the Yalta Conference was in progress, American troops crossed the frontiers of Germany and within a month had crossed the Rhine River.

Then, even as the moment of victory drew near, the Allies suffered a great loss. On April 12, 1945, President Roosevelt died at Warm Springs, Georgia.

Five days later Churchill made a long speech before the House of Commons in which he traced his relationship with the late President. They had exchanged, he said, some seventeen hundred messages and had met nine times, spending in all about one hundred and twenty days in close personal contact. Winston ended with the following words: "For us it remains only to say that in Franklin Roosevelt there died the greatest American friend we have ever known, and the greatest champion of freedom who has ever brought help and comfort from the New World to the Old."

In February of 1945 came the historic Yalta Conference on the Black Sea. The three major participants were Churchill, Roosevelt, and Stalin. It was here that the convening of the United Nations Charter was announced. Roosevelt and Churchill are shown opposite as they have a private conference during the Yalta meetings. Two months later, even as the moment of victory drew near, the Allies suffered a great loss. On April 12, 1945, President Roosevelt died at Warm Springs, Georgia.

The end of German resistance came swiftly in the final weeks of April, 1945. It was preceeded only briefly by the end of Benito Mussolini and Adolf Hitler. Mussolini was captured and shot on April 28 by Italian partisans as he tried to escape to Switzerland before the advancing Allied armies.

Two days later, on April 30, Hitler—who by now had heard of Mussolini's fate—shot himself to death in his underground bunker in Berlin. With him died his bride, Eva Braun, whom he had married only the day before. The bodies of Hitler and his bride were burned in the courtyard above in a ceremony punctuated by the crash of Russian artillery shells.

Admiral Doenitz succeeded Hitler as Germany's leader and immediately set about organizing a surrender. The surrender document was signed at 2:41 a.m. on May 7, 1945, and all fighting stopped at midnight on the eighth of May. Peace had come at last to battered Europe.

"The unconditional surrender of our enemies was the signal for the greatest outburst of joy in the history of mankind, " Churchill remembered. "Weary and worn, impoverished but undaunted and now triumphant, we had a moment that was sublime. We gave thanks to God for the noblest of all His blessings, the sense that we had done our duty."

In July, Churchill met with Premier Stalin and President Truman in Potsdam, a suburb of Berlin, to confer on plans for re-establishing peace. This was to be Winston Churchill's final conference of the war.

It was time now to end the National Coalition government that had served England through five years of war. On July 26, 1945, the results of the general election were announced. The Labour Party under Mr. Clement Attlee had won a decisive victory.

And so it was that Churchill, after ". . . five years and three months of world war . . . all our enemies having surrendered unconditionally or being about to do so, was immediately dismissed by the British electorate from all further conduct of their affairs."

Some two weeks later the Japanese accepted the terms of surrender. World War II was over.

The end of German resistance came swiftly in the final weeks of April, 1945. The surrender document was signed on May 7, and all fighting stopped at midnight on the eighth of May. Peace had come at last to battered Europe. In July, Churchill met with Premier Stalin and President Harry S. Truman in Potsdam, a suburb of Berlin, to confer on plans for re-establishing peace (opposite). This was to be Churchill's final conference of the war. On July 26, 1945, the results of the general election were announced. The Labour party under Mr. Clement Attlee had won a decisive victory. Some two weeks later, the Japanese accepted the terms of surrender. World War II was over.

SEAL OF THE PRESIDENT OF THE U

A Place in History

Many reasons have been offered for Churchill's defeat at the polls in 1945, which to Americans watching from abroad seemed an act of ingratitude. Some say that the voters saw in the Conservative Party a return to the class system. Others felt that the electorate feared a continuation of the severe restrictions imposed by the war. Whatever the reasons for the defeat, it was certainly not meant as a personal rebuke to Winston himself. He had already earned an everlasting place in the hearts of his countrymen.

Britons expected, now that Churchill was seventy, that he would retire to paint pictures, write books, and give the world the benefit of his wisdom as an elder statesman.

But Winston had no intention of retiring. Instead he plunged into the attack against the Labour Government with obvious relish: "I hope you will believe that it is with no personal bias, soreness, or conceit that I declare that the vote of the nation at the general election was one of the greatest disasters that has smitten us in our long and checkered history."

On foreign affairs, Churchill's voice carried more weight than that of any man in England, and perhaps in all the free world. His speech at Fulton, Missouri, in March of 1946, was the beginning of recognition that the "cold war" was on.

Churchill's words roused the world: "From Stettin in the Baltic to Trieste in the Adriatic, an Iron Curtain has descended across the Continent. Behind that line lie all the capitals of the ancient states of Central and Eastern Europe . . . all subject to Soviet control."

Once again came the Churchillian call for strength and courage in the face of threats of force. We had learned the bitter lessons of unpreparedness and appeasement. Winston knew how to handle the Russians: "From what I have seen of our Russian friends and allies during the war I am convinced there is nothing they admire so much as strength and there is nothing they have less respect for than weakness, especially military weakness."

In the meantime, Churchill was busily working on his series of books, *The Second World War*, a magnificent

Churchill had no intention of retiring from public life even though he was no longer Prime Minister. On foreign affairs, his voice carried more weight than that of any man in England, and perhaps in all the free world. His speech at Fulton, Missouri, in March of 1946 (left) was the beginning of recognition that the "cold war" was on. His words roused the world: "From Stettin in the Baltic to Trieste in the Adriatic, an Iron Curtain has descended across the Continent. . . ."

history which would run to six volumes. The first, entitled *The Gathering Storm,* appeared in 1948 and the final volume, *Triumph and Tragedy,* was completed in 1953. The moral of the whole work expressed Winston Churchill's creed: "In War: Resolution; In Defeat: Defiance; In Victory: Magnanimity; In Peace: Goodwill." He was subsequently awarded the Nobel Prize for literature in recognition of this work.

As the century turned the halfway point, Britain's fortunes dipped. The economy suffered as strikes plagued the nation and the pound sterling was devalued from $4.03 to $2.80. Disheartened and discouraged, the people of Great Britain turned once again to the leader who had served them so well in the past. There was reassurance in the familiar, dogged smile beneath the square black hat, and in the sight of Churchill making the V sign from his big, black Humber, and the red, blue, and gold flag of his honorary title—Lord Warden of the Cinque Ports—bravely flying from its hood.

In 1951, with a Conservative victory at the polls, Churchill returned as Prime Minister for the second time. At seventy-six, Churchill was not the man he had been ten years before. His shoulders were rounder; his jowls hung looser beside his bulldog jaws. But his step was still springy, and his eyes could still smolder and twinkle with their old gleam. Friends and enemies alike noticed in Churchill's speech a tendency to slur and meander, but in the heat of this latest campaign, with victory once more within his grasp, the old leader gave no sign of deterioration. And almost from the moment he again took office, British affairs seemed to improve.

In 1952, Winston's old friend, General Dwight Eisenhower, was elected President of the United States. Soon after the new President had taken office, Winston paid a visit to the White House. As in the crucial days of the Second World War, Prime Minister Churchill again enjoyed a warm relationship with an American president.

On February 6 of that year, King George VI died and his daughter Elizabeth ascended to the throne. She was the sixth sovereign Winston had served in his long public life.

On April 24, 1953, Queen Elizabeth knighted Churchill and invested him with the insignia of a Knight Companion of the Most Noble Order of the Garter. He now became Sir Winston Churchill and Clemmie became Lady Churchill. On June 14, 1954, the impressive installation ceremony was held in St. George's Chapel at Windsor Castle. The Order of the Garter is the highest order of chivalry a British citizen can attain and still be eligible to sit in the House of Commons.

In 1951, Churchill returned as Prime Minister for the second time. On April 24, 1953, Queen Elizabeth knighted Churchill and invested him with the insignia of a Knight Companion of the Most Noble Order of the Garter. He became Sir Winston Churchill and his wife became Lady Churchill. On June 14, 1954, the impressive installation ceremony was held in St. George's Chapel at Windsor Castle (opposite).

". . . . no statement or proclamation can enrich his name—the name Sir Winston Churchill is already legend."

By now the years were beginning to take their toll of Sir Winston. It became increasingly evident that the flesh could no longer respond to the command of the vital and undaunted spirit that glowed within him. By the end of 1954 he knew he must soon relinquish the reins of office.

On November 30 of that year, his eightieth birthday, both Houses of Parliament assembled in Westminster Hall to pay him honor. One gift, a portrait by Graham Sutherland, was graciously received—though Churchill would later confess that he did not like the painting. He was also presented with a commemorative book signed by the members of the House of Commons which he would treasure all the rest of his days.

A few months later, on April 5, 1955, Sir Winston Churchill retired from the office of Prime Minister and passed the reins over to his longtime friend and colleague, Mr. Anthony Eden. He still retained his seat in the House from his constituency of Woodford and in the general election of 1959 was re-elected. With his duties as Prime Minister now over, he was able to finish a task he had started many years before—the publication of his four-volume work, *A History of the English-Speaking Peoples.*

On April 9, 1963, Sir Winston was paid the unique honor of being proclaimed an honorary citizen of the United States. President Kennedy read the proclamation in ceremonies at the White House while Sir Winston watched the scene on his television set.

The official proclamation read as follows: "In the dark days and darker nights when Britain stood alone—and most men save Englishmen despaired of England's life—he mobilized the English language and sent it into battle. The incandescent quality of his words illuminated the courage of his countrymen. Given unlimited powers by his fellow citizens, he was ever vigilant to protect their rights. Indifferent himself to danger, he wept over the sorrow of others. A child of the House of Commons, he became in time its father. Accustomed to the hardship of battle, he has no distaste for pleasure. By adding his name to our rolls, we mean to honor him—but his acceptance honors us far more. For no statement or proclamation can enrich his name—the name Sir Winston Churchill is already legend."

By the end of 1954, the years were beginning to take their toll of Sir Winston, and he knew he must soon relinquish the reins of office. On April 5, 1955, he retired and passed the reins over to his longtime friend and colleague, Mr. Anthony Eden. At right, Churchill is shown exactly one month later as he was making a speech at a Conservative party meeting. In 1963, Sir Winston was paid the unique honor of being proclaimed an honorary citizen of the United States.

On May 1, 1963, Sir Winston announced that he was giving up his seat in the House.

In July of 1964, he visited the House of Commons for the last time. By now he was a tired and sick old man who got around in a wheelchair or with the help of others. As the self-styled "child of the House of Commons" left that august chamber for the last time, he paused at the door and turned. Then, thrusting aside two colleagues who were helping him, he managed, with supreme determination, to make the traditional bow to the Speaker of the House. He had made his first bow in this doorway sixty-three years before, during the reign of Queen Victoria.

In January of 1965, Sir Winston came down with a slight cold and was finally put to bed. Shortly thereafter, he suffered a stroke and the dread realization came that the end was near. Gradually the grand old man slipped into a coma but the great heart and the indomitable spirit would not give in. While his family and his nation maintained a quiet vigil, the hours slipped into days until, at last, shortly after eight o'clock in the morning, on Sunday, January 24, 1965, Sir Winston Churchill passed into history. It was the seventy-second anniversary of the death of his father.

The funeral, on January 30, was a stately pageant in which kings and commoners alike gathered together in London to pay final homage to the greatest statesman and national leader of the century—perhaps of all time. Her Majesty, Queen Elizabeth II, broke all precedent to become Britain's first reigning monarch to attend the funeral of a commoner. Churchill was laid to rest beside his mother and father in the quiet village churchyard at Bladon, only a mile from his birthplace at Blenhiem Palace.

Sir Winston Leonard Spencer Churchill's walk with destiny was finished.

In January of 1965, Churchill suffered a stroke, and the dread realization came that the end was near. On January 24, Sir Winston Churchill passed into history. The funeral (right), was held on January 30.

Summary

Some historians have said that had it not been for Winston Churchill, England would not have survived the *Blitz* of 1940–41. No other man of the time, they explain, could have so completely gained the confidence of the British people. No one can deny that the margin of survival was small. That slender difference between victory and defeat could very well have been the presence of Winston Churchill at No. 10 Downing Street.

His whole life prior to becoming Prime Minister had been, he felt, but a preparation for that crucial hour in 1940. As a child he had been largely ignored by his parents. Sent away to a boy's school, he soon developed the characteristics that would later mark Churchill the man: independence, unbending stubbornness, and tenacity.

As a youth he watched with pride as his rather cold and remote father joined in the cut and thrust of parliamentary debate in the House of Commons. He liked to refer to himself as a "child of the House of Commons." For more than half a century, both in power and in loyal opposition, he enjoyed and respected the traditions and responsibilities of parliamentary government.

As a soldier of the queen he tasted the hot excitement of battle and danger. As a newspaper correspondent and writer he learned the power of the written word and the ethics of responsible journalism. Always a loyal subject of the Crown, he served two queens and four kings in a variety of posts. Given sweeping powers by his countrymen, he was ever zealous to protect their rights. As a painter he could capture the beauty of a scene with tenderness and color. But in the ugly face of tyranny and despotism he could be ruthless and defiant.

In that most fateful hour of English history, Winston Churchill stepped forward to meet his destiny with confidence. When the odds were greatest and the fate of England hung in the balance, there appeared amid the chaos the determined scowl of Winston Churchill—fingers thrust aloft in the sign of a V for victory. Above the din of exploding bombs and crashing buildings, there sounded a clarion call to duty—a defiant voice that echoed the traditions of Nelson, Marlborough, and Wellington.

"We shall not flag or fail . . . We shall never surrender . . . Victory; no matter how long or hard the road may be . . ."

England heard the call and answered the challenge. Winston Churchill focused the spotlight of history upon the courage and determination of his people. And, illuminated by his words, England's darkest hour became, indeed, "Their Finest Hour!"

Bibliography

ADLER, BILL, ed. *The Churchill Wit.* New York: Coward-McCann, 1965.

ADAMIC, LOUIS. *Dinner at the White House.* New York: Harper, 1961.

AYLING, S. E. *Portraits in Power.* New York: Barnes and Noble, 1963.

BERKENHEAD, FREDERICK. *The Professor and the Prime Minister.* Boston: Houghton Mifflin, 1962.

BERLIN, ISAIAH. *Mr. Churchill in 1940.* Boston: Houghton Mifflin, 1964.

BIBESCO, MARTHE. *Sir Winston Churchill.* New York: John Day, 1959.

BLAKE, ROBERT. *Unrepentant Tory.* New York: St. Martins Press.

BOCCA, GEOFFREY. *The Adventurous Life of Winston Churchill.* New York: Messner, 1958.

BONHAM-CARTER, VIOLET (LADY ASQUITH). *Winston Churchill, An Intimate Portrait.* New York: Harcourt, 1965.

BROAD, LEWIS. *Winston Churchill.* New York: Hawthorn, 1958.

BROMAGE, M. *Churchill and Ireland.* Notre Dame, Indiana: University of Notre Dame Press, 1964.

BRYANT, ARTHUR. *Turn of the Tide.* New York: Doubleday.

CHURCHILL, JOHN SPENCER. *A Churchill Canvas.* Boston: Little, Brown.

CHURCHILL, RANDOLPH, ed. *Churchill: His Life in Photographs.* New York: Rinehart, 1955.

———. *Winston S. Churchill. Youth, 1874-1900.* New York: Houghton Mifflin, 1966.

CHURCHILL, WINSTON. *Frontiers and Wars;* his first four books edited into one volume. (*London to Ladysmith; The River War; The Malakand Field Force; Ian Hamilton's March*). New York: Harcourt, 1962.

———. *Savrola,* novel. London, 1900.

———. *Mr. Broderick's Army.* London, 1903.

———. *Lord Randolph Churchill* (2 vols.). London: Odhams, 1952.

CHURCHILL, WINSTON. *My African Journey.* London: Holland, 1908.

———. *The World Crisis* (5 vols.). New York: Scribner, 1923-31.

———. *My Early Life.* New York: Scribner, 1958.

———. *The Unknown War.* London, 1931.

———. *Thoughts and Adventures.* London, 1932.

———. *Marlborough, His Life and Times* (4 vols.). New York: Scribner, 1933.

———. *Great Contemporaries.* New York: Putnam, 1937.

———. *Step by Step, 1936-1939.* New York: Putnam, 1939.

———. *Painting as a Pastime.* New York: Whittlesey House, 1950.

———. *The Second World War* (6 vols.). Boston: Houghton Mifflin, 1948-53.

———. *History of the English Speaking Peoples* (4 vols.). New York: Dodd, Mead, 1965.

———. *The American Civil War.* New York: Dodd, Mead, 1961.

———. *The Island Race.* New York: Dodd, Mead, 1964.

———. *Blood, Sweat and Tears, Speeches.* New York: Putnam, 1941.

———. *Dawn of Liberation, War Speeches.* Boston: Little, Brown, 1943.

———. *Europe Unite, Speeches.* Boston: Houghton Mifflin, 1950.

———. *In The Balance, Speeches 1949-50.* Boston: Houghton Mifflin, 1951.

———. *Victory, War Speeches.* Boston: Little, Brown, 1946.

———. *Churchill Reader.* New York: Houghton Mifflin, 1954.

———. *Maxims and Reflections.* Boston: Houghton Mifflin, 1947.

———. *Winston Churchill, A Self-Portrait from his Own Words.* London: Eyre, 1954.

COOLIDGE, OLIVIA. *Winston Churchill and the Story of Two World Wars.* Boston: Houghton Mifflin, 1960.

COWLES, VIRGINIA. *Winston Churchill: The Era and the Man.* New York: Universal Library, 1954.

DE MENDELSSOHN, PETER. *The Age of Churchill.* New York: Knopf, 1961.

EADE, CHARLES, ed. *Churchill by his Contemporaries.* New York: Simon & Schuster, 1953.

FARRELL, ALAN. *Sir Winston Churchill.* London: Faber, 1962.

FISHMAN, JACK. *My Darling Clementine.* New York: Macmillan, 1963.

GRAEBNER, WALTER. *My Dear Mr. Churchill.* Boston: Houghton Mifflin, 1965.

GUEDALLA, PHILIP. *Mr. Churchill.* New York: Reynal & Hitchcock, 1942.

HARRITY, RICHARD, ed. *Man of the Century.* New York: Duell, Sloan & Pearce, 1962.

HEATH, F. W., ed. *Great Destiny.* New York: Putnam, 1965.

HIGGINS, TRUMBULL. *Winston Churchill and the Second Front.* New York: Oxford University Press, 1957.

HOWELLS, ROY. *Churchill's Last Years.* New York: McKay, 1966.

HUGHES, EMRYS. *Winston Churchill, British Bulldog.* New York: Exposition, 1955.

KRAUSS, RENE. *Winston Churchill.* New York: Lippincott, 1941.

______. *Winston Churchill in the Mirror.* New York: Dutton, 1944.

LESLIE, ANITA. *The Fabulous Leonard Jerome.*

LE VIEN, JACK, and JOHN LORD. *Winston Churchill: The Valiant Years.* New York: Geis, 1962.

London *Times*, eds. *The Churchill Years, 1874-1965.* New York: Viking, 1965.

MCGOWAN, NORMAN. *My Years With Churchill.* New York, 1958.

MOOREHEAD, ALAN. *Winston Churchill.* New York: Viking, 1960.

______. *Winston Churchill in Trial and Triumph.* Boston: Houghton Mifflin, 1955.

MORAN, CHARLES. *Churchill: Taken from the Diaries of Lord Moran.* Cambridge, Massachusetts: Houghton Mifflin, 1966.

MORIN, RELMAN. *Churchill.* Englewood, New Jersey: Prentice-Hall, 1965.

MORTON, HENRY. *Atlantic Meeting.* New York: Dodd, Mead, 1943.

NEL, ELIZABETH. *Mr. Churchill's Secretary.* New York: Coward-McCann, 1958.

New York *Times*, eds. *Churchill in Memorium.* New York: Bantam, 1965.

PAWLE, GERALD. *The War and Colonel Warden.* New York: Knopf, 1963.

Readers Digest, eds. *Man of the Century.* Boston: Little, Brown, 1965.

ROBERTS, CECIL. *A Man Arose.* New York: Macmillan, 1941.

ROWSE, ALFRED. *The Early Churchills: An English Family.* New York: Harper, 1956.

______. *The Story of the Churchills from the death of Marlborough to present.*

SHERIDAN, CLARE. *Naked Truth.* New York: Harper & Row.

STEWART, HERBERT. *Winged Words.* New York: Bouregy, 1954.

TAYLOR, ROBERT LEWIS. *Winston Churchill.* New York: Doubleday, 1952.

THOMPSON, MALCOM. *Churchill, His Life and Times.* London: Odhams, 1965.

THOMPSON, REGINALD. *Winston Churchill.* New York: Doubleday, 1963.

THOMPSON, WALTER. *Assignment: Churchill.* New York: Farrar, Straus, 1955.

WIBBERLEY, LEONARD. *The Life of Winston Churchill.* New York: (Ariel) Farra, Straus, 1956.

WOODS, FREDERICK. *Bibliography of the Works of Sir Winston Churchill.* Toronto, Canada: University of Toronto Press, 1963.

Index

Acknowledgments: Photographs on pages 2-3, 8-9, 10-11, 18 (left), 30-31, 35, 52 (bottom, left), 54, 56, 63, 65, 66-67, 70, 74-75, 80-81, 83, 85, 86-87, and 89 from the files of Wide World Photos, Inc.; photograph on page 15 (top), The Bettman Archive; photograph on page 15 (bottom), Aerofilms Limited; photograph on page 17, Culver Pictures, Inc.; photographs on pages 21, 24-25, 27, 36-37, 39, 50 (top), and 52 (top), Radio Times Hulton Picture Library; photographs on pages 46-47 and 77, Imperial War Museum; photograph on page 18 (right), "Paris Match"; photograph on page 23, Mirrorpic; photograph on pages 40-41, P.A.—Reuter Photos, Ltd.; photograph on page 50 (bottom), Central Press; photograph on page 52 (bottom, right), London News Agency Photos Ltd.; photograph on pages 60-61, Mr. Cecil Beaton; photograph on page 78, Camera Press. Illustrations on pages 13, 32-33, 35, 43, 51, 58-59, 68-69, and 73 by Bob Brunton, Hollis Associates; illustrations on pages 28-29, 42, 44-45, 48-49, and 90 by Nita Engle, Hollis Associates.